PARIS 360°

2003 Herausgegeben in Deutschland von
Verlag Karl Müller GmbH
Venloer Str. 1271, 50829 Köln
Tel.: 0049- 0221-13065-0
Fax: 0049- 0221-13065-210

Druck: Juni 2003, Tipografia Valdostana / Aoste, Italy

ISBN 3-89893-116-1

PARIS 360°

Text / Jacques Meunier
Fotos / Attilio Boccazzi-Varotto
+ Enrico Formica
Zeichnungen / Luisa Romussi
Historische und Kunstgeschichtliche Recherchen
Hervé Juvin

KARL MÜLLER

Text
Jacques Meunier

Reisen, die einem das andere Ende der Welt in Aussicht stellen, sind müßig. Das Ende der Welt ist überall. Ob man es als entferntesten Punkt auf der Erde oder im Weltraum bezeichnet, es ist es stets hinter dem Rücken. Man sollte seine Zeit jedoch nicht damit verschwenden, sich umzusehen. Das Ende der Welt dreht sich mit und atmet einem wiederum in den Nacken.

Diese Seite der Illusion ist das Ende eines Landes ebenso wie ein Gefühl, ein topographischer John O'Groats, wie eine innere Dimension. Ein Ort, an dem es kein Dahinter mehr gibt, an dem jeder ein Einmann-Tete-a-Tete genießt. Die Spanier mit ihrer Neigung zum Nihilismus machen keinen Unterschied zwischen dem Ende der Welt und dem Untergang der Welt. In Ushuaia in Feuerland ist ein Ferngespräch eine wahre Herausforderung, weil Horden von Schmarotzern, die nach einer Möglichkeit zum kostenlosen Telefonieren suchen, die öffentlichen Telefonzellen belagern. Hier hat ein findiger Ladenbesitzer eine »boutique de téléphones« eröffnet, genannt »Telefonzelle am Ende der Welt«. Wenn man indiskret sein möchte, was kaum tadelnswert ist, wie jeder betont, hört man ganz sicher etwas wie: »Hallo, Liebling! Ich bin's. Ich bin in Ushuaia und rufe dich vom Ende der Welt an, das stimmt natürlich nicht ganz, ich spreche von der unteren Seite der Erde.«

Schön und gut, mag man jetzt denken, aber was hat das alles mit diesem Buch zu tun? Ich will es zu erklären versuchen, wenn auch um den Preis einer Antipodenübung, ein gewagter Sprung in das Reich des Lesens, der Bilder und der Erinnerungen.

Forschung in Verbindung mit der extremen und der mittelmäßigen Ethnographie mündet oftmals im Wesentlichen. Meine langen Reisen haben mir »mein« Paris näher gebracht, weil ich überall, ob in Amazonien oder der Antarktis, auf den Philippinen oder in Bengalen, in New York oder Kirgisien, begierig nach dem Eiffelturm und dem Champs-Élysées gefragt wurde, nach den Bistros und den Frauen von Paris, nach Notre-Dame und der Seine. Am Orinoko zeigte mir einmal ein Venezueler einen Videofilm, den er den vier Jahreszeiten in Paris gewidmet hatte. Wir tranken einen Bordeaux, der im Begriff war, in einen Madeira überzugehen, und betrachteten den Schnee, der auf den Dôme des Invalides fiel, während der Kommentator sich in einem aussichtslosen Kampf mit dem metallischen Rauschen des Bambus und der Palmen maß. Am Ende der Welt waren wir von dem verzückt, was mein Gastgeber für sein Herz hielt. Sein Paris war eine Metapher und er sprach davon, wie die Indianer von ihren Mythen sprechen. Star dieses wundervollen Abends war ein bunter Ara, dem mein Gastgeber beigebracht hatte, »Vive la France!« zu krächzen. Der Vogel – schüchtern vielleicht oder gerissen – zögerte diese Glanzleistung hinaus, bis seine Stimmbänder mit einer halben Packung Petit Fours richtig geölt waren.

Paris lebt in Bildern. Filme, Romane und Lieder erscheinen vor dem geistigen Auge. Zola, Hugo, Baudelaire, Balzac, Aragon, Henry Miller, Cendrars, Léo Malet und Perec sind noch immer geläufige Namen. Die Anthologien bieten François Villon, Louis-Sébastien Mercier, Restif de la Bretonne, Gérard de Nerval, Paul Léautaud, Léon-Paul Fargue, Simenon und Modiano. Andere werden notgedrungen vernachlässigt. Keinen Zutritt haben außerdem Maler und Fotografen, deren Name Legion lautet. Toulouse-Lautrec und Utrillo erfanden den Montmartre: Carco, Mac Orlan und Dorgelès fanden darin ihre Wahrheit. Andere, diskretere, loben ihre Straßen, ihre Bars, ihre Kinos oder ihre Kabaretts. All diese Bilder formen ein Gebäude, das niemanden ausschließt, niemanden für unwürdig erklärt.

Paris lädt sich selbst ein und multipliziert sich in all unseren Kreuz- und Querblicken. Das unbedeutendste Gedicht trägt ein wenig zu seiner Jugend bei. Als ich ein Junge war, lebte ich etwa 50 km stromaufwärts von der Hauptstadt. Ich warf Treibgut in die Seine und beobachtete, wie es davongetragen wurde mit dem leichten Herzen desjenigen, dessen Ritual vollbracht ist. Meine Religion war vollkommen. Eines Tages würde ich nach Paris gehen. Auf dem Nachhauseweg wiederholte ich wie im Gebet den mnemotechnischen Jingle, der mir half, mich an die Städte am Fluss zu erinnern: »Trois melons paresseux roulaient vers le

Havre.« Hinter dieser ehrwürdigen Formel verbargen sich die Namen Troyes, Melun, Paris, Rouen und Le Havre. Wissenschaft und Surrealismus zeigten bereits auf den Horizont.

André Breton, Philippe Soupault, Robert Desnos, Jacques Prévert, Raymond Queneau. Die Liste der Surrealisten oder surrealistischen Dichter, die Paris methodisch erforschten und in ein Kreuzworträtsel verwandelten (ein Magnetfeld zufälliger Begegnungen und Illuminationen), trägt den Stempel einer radikalen Spaltung. Man muss alles, was zwischen »Nadja« (1928) und »Zazie dans le métro« (1959) geschrieben wurde, noch einmal lesen, um zu verstehen, wie es dazu kam und weshalb man nicht länger das Gefühl hat, bei Paris zu leben, sondern in Paris.

Die Surrealisten haben die Stadt in eine allgemein gültige Ordnung umgewandelt, eine Ökumene, in der sich jedes Detail wie das Bruchstück eines Hologramms auf das Ganze bezieht. Streng genommen haben sie Paris neu erfunden und ihre Wandergedichte, ihre Sehnsucht nach Ekstase und plötzlicher Erleuchtung sind den Buschgesängen trügerisch ähnlich, mit denen die Aborigines ihre Wüsten bevölkert haben, Gesänge, die sie gemäß ihren Vorlieben für Einweihungszwecke außer Acht lassen. Surrealisten können nicht nur einflussreich, sondern auch unbeschwert sein. Auf Aragons »Le paysan de Paris« aus dem Jahr 1926 folgte vier oder fünf Jahre später folgender frivoler Knittelvers:

»Bordel pour bordel	*»Bordell für Bordell*
j'aime mieux le métro	*ich ziehe die Métro vor,*
c'est moins cher	*dort ist es billiger*
et c'est bien plus chaud.«	*und viel wärmer.«*

Ein gelehrteres Angebot stammt aus der Feder von André Breton, dessen »L'amour fou« (1937) die gekünstelte Annäherung an den Tagesablauf eines Menschen umfasst. »Unser tägliches Leben, was noch wichtiger ist, hält kleine Entdeckungen jener Art im Überfluss bereit ..., Entdeckungen die ich letztendlich für unbedeutend halte. Ich bin absolut überzeugt, dass alle Wahrnehmungen ... in sich selbst die Lösung tragen, symbolisch oder anders, eine Schwierigkeit, der man sich ganz allein stellen muss. Es läuft einfach darauf hinaus, dass man im Labyrinth seinen Weg findet. Der verrückte Drang zu interpretieren, beginnt dort, wo der unvorbereitete Beobachter vor diesem Wald der Symbole erschrickt.«

Mit solchen Tipps im Kopf machte ich mich kürzlich daran, die Ethnologie einer parisischen Straße (der Rue de Buci) zu bestimmen und anschließend explorierte ich die Dächer von Paris soziologisch. Beide Unternehmen hatten eine parodistische, beinahe ironische Färbung, doch Ziel war es, wenn auch nicht offensichtlich, den Puls der Stadt zu fühlen. Ich versuchte, mich zu distanzieren, damit ich fähig war, von der schmucklosen Exotik meines eigenen Milieus überrascht zu werden. Es war einfacher, sich das auszudenken, als es zu verwirklichen. Ich musste mich in die Lage dessen versetzen, der Paris zum ersten Mal entdeckt, damit ich Orte und Gebäude, Plätze und Passanten, den Bahnhof, die Métro, Kirchen, die Menge und die Ladenbesitzer mit den Augen eines anderen sah. Ich musste Einfachheit und Unschuld wiederentdecken, die Vorstellung mit einem Achselzucken abtun, dass Dinge sich um sich selbst drehen und einfach so sind, wie sie sind. Ich musste das geschäftige Treiben der Stadt verlassen und mich an das Stillschweigen heranmachen, das Verstohlene und das Ungesagte. Dank meiner langen Auslandsreisen fiel mir dies leichter, denn sie erlaubten mir nach meiner Rückkehr, die Welt in der ich lebte, misstrauisch zu betrachten. Weshalb sind Ampeln rot? Warum schreiben wir auf DIN-A4-Papier? Sind Adressbücher und -karteien ein Ersatz für die Erinnerung an Stammbäume? Beruht die Art, wie der Kellner in einem Café seine Bestellung aufnimmt, auf einem traditionellen Know-how oder einer sehr alten Wissenschaft? Hat jede Straße einen eigenen Klang? Ihre eigene sichtbare Ökologie? Welche Merkmale ordnet jemand einem Bezirk zu? So viele Fragen, die mich nach und nach tief in das Mysterium Paris zogen und mich zu einer Schlussfolgerung veranlassten, die nicht allzu weit entfernt ist von jener, die der Prähistoriker André Leroi-Gourhan gegen Ende seines Lebens ausdrückt: »Wenn wir nach der Menschheit suchen, suchen wir nach uns selbst. Jede unserer Theorien ist eine Art Selbstporträt.«

Im Sommer dachte ich über die Dächer von Paris nach. Es war heiß. Ein junges Mädchen hatte ein Badetuch ausgebreitet und sonnte sich. Weiter entfernt demontierte ein Heizer einen Schornstein und an einem Fenstersims ließ sich eine akrobatische Concierge von ihrer Beleibtheit nicht davon abhalten, ihre Wäsche im Freien aufzuhängen. Mir kam die glänzende Idee, über dieses Leben auf den Dächern, die von mehr Menschen bevölkert waren, als ich mir vorgestellt hatte, eine Radioreportage zu machen. Ich hängte mir meinen Kassettenrekorder um und machte mich an die Arbeit.

Die Ausbeute? Ein Imker, zwei Feuerwehrleute auf Inspektionstour, ein Ingenieur, ein Fassadenkletterer, ein Künstler, Bauarbeiter, ein paar Kinder, ein paar Filmfreunde und ein paar Träumer. In dieser kleinen Welt versteckte sich ein anderes Paris. Das Intermezzo gewährte mir Einblick in eine Stadt, die hinter der Stadt verborgen lag, die ich kannte. Ich entdeckte sogar etwa 15 Pavillons auf dem Dach einer Garage, an einem Ort, der als »Klein-Russland« bekannt ist, denn hier lebten jahrelang russische Taxifahrer.

Ich unternahm mehrere Exkursionen in die Katakomben von Paris, um die Stadt vollkommen kennen zu lernen. Von dort stammen die folgenden aphoristischen Worte:

»Mieux	»Es ist besser,
vaut être	ein Höhlenbewohner
un spéléologue	ohne Höhle
qu'un homme	zu sein
sans profondeur.«	als ein Mensch ohne Tiefe.«

Hier lügt Paris. Ein gigantisches Kreuzworträtsel mit unendlichen Feldern. Tausendundeine Promenade würden nicht ausreichen, sie alle auszufüllen. Ich kenne das alles zu gut. Trotzdem ist es eine gute Idee herumzuschlendern und einige Wortfetzen aufzuschnappen. Jeder von uns Parisern auf seine Weise. Ein Ballon Beaujolais, das Gelb der Briefkästen und das Blau einer Packung Gitanes haben hier mehr Gewicht als andernorts.

Am Samstag, den 10. Juni 1995, haben wir um 16:05 Uhr die Rue Marcel Duchamp eingeweiht. Reden, Fanfaren und Majoretten. Die Ortsansässigen hatten etwa 100 Quadrate 1 m x 1 m markiert, in denen jeder, dem danach war, Künstler oder nicht, den großen alten Herrn des Surrealismus ehren konnte, den Vater des Readymade, der 1968 verstorben war. Andréa Cohen spielte auf dem Pianoakkordeon Stücke von John Cage. Krönung des Abends war Musik von den Antillen. Das naive Fest einer Straße, die seit langem mit der offiziellen Bezeichnung CC13 belastet war, eine tolle Party à la Prévert, das Lachen der Kinder übertönte so viel Wertloses. Es besteht berechtigter Zweifel, ob all das in Einklang mit dem Surrealismus stand, ob die Marseillaise, die zu Ehren Duchamps gespielt wurde, nach seinem Geschmack war, ob die Worte des Ministers angemessen waren. Teeny, die Witwe Duchamps, beobachtete das Treiben vom Rollstuhl aus. Die Thermik, verursacht durch die Reihen der Hochhäuser, die das letzte Refugium niedriger Häuser finster betrachten, hob Plastiktüten in den Himmel wie eine Schwadron Heißluftballons.

Dieses Buch fügt jedem Paris, das ich entdeckt habe, eine neue Dimension hinzu. Es ist eine Rückbesinnung auf das Vertraute über die Gesamtheit. Es berührt die Sinne und erweckt Visionen. Ich weiß nicht, weshalb: Es erinnert mich an jene Momente der Expansion, jene ewigen Augenblicke, wenn das Ende der Welt, das nahe und das ferne, zum Herzen der Welt wird.

Idle indeed are the journeys that dangle before you the far ends of the earth. The terminus of the world is everywhere. If one calls it the furthest point on the planet or in space, one being round, the other curved, why it's just behind your back. But don't waste time turning to see. The end of the world would swing round with you and, hey presto, it'd be right there breathing down your neck once again.

This flip side of your illusions is as much a Land's End as a feeling, a topographical John O'Groats as an interior dimension. A place where there is no longer a beyond, where everyone can enjoy a one-man tête-à-tête. The Spanish with their penchant for nihilism draw no distinction between the world's end and the end of the world. At Ushuaia in Tierra del Fuego, where making a long-distance call is a herculean task, since the hotels charge the earth and the public booths are besieged by hordes of scroungers looking for ways to make a free call, a crafty shopkeeper has opened a «boutique de téléphones» called the «end of the world telephone box». If you've a mind to be indiscreet, though it's hardly a sin as everyone shouts like crazy, you'll be bound to hear such oddities as «Hello, dear. It's me. I'm at Ushuaia and I'm phoning you from the end of the world, well, not exactly, I mean the bottom bit of the earth».

Fair enough, you'll be thinking, but what's it all got to do with Paris 360°? Let me try and explain, albeit at the price of an antipodean exercise, a perilous leap into the area of readings, pictures and memories.

Research allied with the extreme and run-of-the-mill ethnography often debouch into the essential. My long journeys have taught me «my» Paris, since, provincial though I am, I have everywhere been plied, whether in Amazonia or the Antarctic, in the Philippines or Bengal, whether in New York or Kirghistan, with eager questions about the Eiffel Tower and the Champs Elysées. Paris's bistros and its women. Notre-Dame and the Seine. Once, beside the Orinoco, a Venezuelan showed me a video film devoted to Paris in the four seasons. As we sipped some Bordeaux that was in the process of changing its label to become Madeira, we watched the snow descend on the Dôme des Invalides, while the voice of the commentator, duly swathed in the strains from Vivaldian violins, fought a losing battle with the metallic rustling of the bamboo plants and the palms. We at the far end of the world were entranced with what my host regarded as its heart. His Paris had thus the value of a metaphor and he told it like the Indians tell their myths. The star turn of this enchanting evening was provided by a gaily-coloured macaw, which my host had taught to cry «Vive la France!». Shy, perhaps, or canny to a fault, the enterprising bird delayed its execution of this tour de force until its vocal cords had been duly greased with hay a box of petits fours. Its Francophony had clearly become its stock-in-trade.

The stuff of Paris lies in its representations. Films, novels and songs come to mind. Zola, Hugo, Baudelaire, Balzac, Aragon, Henry Miller, Cendrars, Léo Malet and Perec are names that still haunt a host of quarters. The anthologies offer François Villon, Louis-Sébastien Mercier, Restif de la Bretonne, Gérard de Nerval, Paul Léautaud, Leon-Paul Fargue, Simenon and Modiano. Others are perforce omitted. No entry, either, must be the decision for the painters and photographers, since their name is Legion. Toulouse-Lautrec and Utrillo invented Montmartre: Carco, Mac Orlan and Dorgelès found their truth therein. Others, more discreet, eulogised their streets, their bars, their cinemas or their cabarets. All these pictures form a pile in which none is excluded, none annulled.

Paris invents herself and multiplies in all these criss-cross glances of ours. The meanest poem adds its mite to her youth. When I was a boy and lived some 50 kilometres upstream from the capital, I used to go and cast flotsam into the Seine, somewhat after the manner of the Hindu by his Ganges, and watch it drift away with the light heart of one whose ritual has been accomplished. My religion was complete. One day, I would go to Paris. And when I went home, I used to recite like a prayer the mnemonic jingle that helped me to remember the string of towns beside the river: «Trois melons paresseux roulaient vers le Havre»: Troyes, Melun, Paris, Rouen and Le Havre were the names hidden in this hoary old formula. Science and surrealism were already pointing towards the horizon.

André Breton, Philippe Soupault, Robert Desnos, Jacques Prévert, Raymond Queneau. The list of surrealist or surrealisting poets whose methodical driftings explored Paris and transformed it into a vast crossword puzzle territory (a magnetic field of coincidences, encounters and illuminations) bears the stamp of a radical cleavage. One would have to reread everything written between «Nadja» (1928) and «Zazie dans le métro» (1959) to understand how this took place, and how, surreptitiously, we had no longer the feeling of living at Paris, but in Paris.

The surrealists have converted the city into a generalised order, an «oikoumene», where each detail, like a fragment of a hologram, refers back to the whole. Strictly speaking, they have reinvented Paris, and their walkabout poems, their yen for trances and satori (sudden enlightment) are deceptively similar to the bush chants with which the Australian aboriginals have peopled their deserts, chants that they set aside, each according to his likes, for initiatory purposes.

The surrealists could be both weighty and light-hearted. Aragon's «Le paysan de Paris» in 1926 had been preceded some four or five years earlier by this flippant doggerel:

«Bordel pour bordel	*«'Twixt bawdlam*
j'aime mieux le métro	*and bedlam I'd chose the Metro*
c'est moins cher	*it's cheaper and much warmer*
et c'est bien plus chaud».	*ever so»*

A more learned offering comes from the pen of André Breton, whose «L'amour fou» (1937) contains this mannered approach to the passing of one's day. Its tone hovers between the esoteric and the ethnological. «Our daily life, what is more, abounds in little discoveries of the kind where a touch of apparent gratuitousness frequently predominates, this in all probability being a function of our momentary lack of comprehension, discoveries that I find in the end to be among the least negligible. I am firmly persuaded that all perceptions recorded in the least voluntary manner such, for example, as that of words thrown out for all and sundry, bear within themselves the solution, symbolic or otherwise, of a difficulty one has to face unaided. It simply amounts to being able to find one's way in the labyrinth. The mad urge to interpret only begins where the unprepared observer takes fright in these forêts de symboles. Yet I maintain that attention would sooner see itself brought to naught than lend itself for a second, on behalf of a being to which the desire of such being remains external».

With these counsels in mind, I recently set out to determine the ethnology of a Parisian street (the Rue de Buci), and then on a sociological exploration of the roofs of Paris. These two enterprises had a parodying, almost ironical slant, but their aim, albeit not apparent, was to take the city's pulse. My concern was to defamiliarise myself as to be able to take by surprise the unadorned exoticism of my own surroundings.

Easier to excogitate than to execute. It would be necessary to put myself in the shoes of someone discovering Paris for the first time, to look at these places and buildings, these squares and passers-by, this station, that metro, these churches, that crowd and those shop keepers through another's eyes. It was necessary to rediscover simplicity and innocence, to shrug off the notion that things run on their own and that they are just as they are, to step aside from the city's hustle and bustle to get down to the tacit, the furtive, the implicit and the left unsaid. This was rendered easier by my long journeys abroad which allowed me on my return to look askance at the unquestioned world in which I live. Why are traffic lights red? Why do we write on paper measuring 297x210 mm? What's the tipping system? Are address books and mailing lists a substitute for the remembering of family trees? Can smoking a single cigarette be likened to a «small crematory sacrifice»? Does the way a café waiter notes his orders stem from a traditional know-how or some very ancient science? Does each and every street have a particular «sound print»? Its own visual ecology? What are the signs that one belongs to a district? So many questions that gradually drew me deep into the mystery of Paris and brought me to a conclusion not so very far from that which the prehistorian André Leroi-Gourhan expressed towards the end of his life: «When we look for man, we are searching for ourselves. Each of our theories is something of a self-portrait».

One summer, cut off from my ethnological haunts, I was contemplating the

Parisian roofscape. It was hot and a young girl had spread a beach towel out on the bare metal to sunbathe. Further off a boilerman was dismantling a chimney, while an acrobatic concierge on a ledge was not letting her embonpoint prevent her from hanging out her washing. The idea came to me that this tin-roof land, more densely peopled that I had imagined, might make the subject of a radio reportage. I explored this forest canopy with my tape-recorder on my back.

My close encounters? A beekeeper in the XIIIème, two firemen on a tour of inspection, an engineer taking pollution readings, a cat-burglar who did not stop to pass the time of day, an artist striving to fit the whole gamut of greys into an abstract painting, building workers, some kids putting their head for heights to the test by walking along the gutters at sunset, some buffs watching the Opera's rehearsals for free, and some dreamers star-gazing amid forbidden fumes. All this little world told of the discovery of an unproclaimed Paris. An archipelago Paris for these new treetop barons. A surreal Paris, the night.

This intermezzo on the roofs gave me a glimpse of a town hidden above the one I knew. I even discovered fifteen or so pavilions on the roof of a garage at a place known as «Little Russia», since it was for many years the home of Russian taxidrivers. To get to know Paris from the basement to the attic, I also made several excursions into its catacombs, whence, for ever faithful to the surrealist objective, I drew this aphoristic screed:

«Mieux	«Better it is
vaut être	to be
un spéléologue	a surficial, caveless
sans grottes	caver
qu'un homme	than to be
sans profondeur».	a superficial man».

There, then, lies Paris. A gigantic crossword puzzle with interminable lights. A thousand and one promenades would not suffice to fill them all. I know this all too well. Even so, it's a good idea to idle along and pick up some scraps of conversation. Each of us parisianises after his or her fashion. A balloon of Beaujolais, the yellow of the letter-boxes and the blue of a packet of Gitanes have more weight here than elsewhere.

On Saturday the tenth of June, 1995, at five past four in the afternoon, we inaugurated Rue Marcel Duchamp. Speeches, fanfares and majorettes. The locals had marked out a hundred or so one by one metre squares on the pavement where those who felt so inclined, whether artists or not, were fully free to render their homage to this Grand Old Man of surrealism, father of the ready-made, who died in 1968. Andréa Cohen played pieces by John Cage, Jean Demeaux, on the piano accordion, and the somewhat nippy evening was rounded off to the strains of music from the Antilles. Naive kermis of a street that had long been saddled with the official title CC13, popular high jinks à la Prévert, the laughter of children excited over so much bric-à-brac. A legitimate doubt whether all this was in line with the right way of surrealism, whether the Marseillaise played in Duchamp's honor was exactly to his taste, whether the minister's words were quite apropos. «Tant pis».

Teeny, Duchamp's widow, watched the junketing from the depths of her wheelchair. I saw her leave with her cowboy coiffure, swaying, pushed by chicites. The thermals generated by the rows of high-rises that frown over this last little eyot of low houses swept plastic bags skywards like a squadron of hot-air ballons.

Paris 360° adds a new dimension to all these Parises I have just evoked. Photos show what people would never get to see, short of being whirling dervishes or four-headed kings, like the one on the top of the Bayon complex at Angkor. Paris 360° is a «renvoi» to the intimate via the totality. It knocks one's senses out of kilter and one's vision out of joint. It reminds me of those moments in expansion, those eternal instants, when the corners of the world, both the nearest and the farthest, become its one heart.

Fotos Photographs

Attilio Boccazzi-Varotto Enrico Formica

1.

2.

3.

LA GEODE

LE PONT - NEUF

PALAIS BOURBON

LE SACRE - COEUR

CATHEDRALE DE NOTRE DAME

4.

5.

1.
Wappen von Paris am Gitter des Petit Palais.
Emblem of Paris on the gate of the Petit Palais.

2.
Blick auf Paris von der Terrasse der 4. Bezirkspräfektur. Im Vordergrund die Ile St-Louis.
Panorama of Paris from the terrace of the Prefecture of the 4th Arrondissement with the Ile St-Louis.

6. ▶

3.
Vorplatz von Notre-Dame.
The square in front of Notre-Dame.

4.
Turmspitze der Sainte-Chapelle.
Spire of the Sainte-Chapelle.

5.
Quai des Orfèvres vom Pont St-Michel aus gesehen.
Quai des Orfèvres seen from the Pont St-Michel.

6.
Ausflugsboot auf der Seine, zwischen Ile de la Cité und linkem Ufer.
Water-bus on the Seine between the Ile de la Cité and the Rive Gauche.

7.
Hôtel de Ville und Place de l'Hôtel de Ville, von der Ecke Rue de Rivoli/Rue du Renard aus aufgenommen.
The City Hall and its square seen from the corner between the Rue de Rivoli and the Rue du Renard.

8.
Tour St-Jacques.

9.
Teil der Glasgalerie im Forum des Halles.
A detail of the glass gallery in Les Halles.

10./11.
Beaubourg: Wasserspiele des Stravinsky-Brunnens mit kinetischen Kunstwerken von Tinguely und Nikki de St-Phalle.
Beaubourg: jeux d'eau in the Stravinsky fountain, with mobiles by Tinguely and Nikki de St-Phalle.

12.
Beaubourg: Centre Pompidou und Esplanade.
Beaubourg: the Georges Pompidou Centre and its esplanade.

13.
Kontrastierende Epochen und Stile in der Rue de Rennes.
Contrasting styles and periods along the Rue de Rennes.

14.
Die Kirche St-Sulpice.
St Sulpice Church.

15.
Ein Abschnitt des Luxemburger Gartens.
A glimpse of the Luxembourg Gardens.

8.

9.

◀10.
11.

12.

LE MONT LOZERE
salon de thé

13.

fnac
LIVRES
DISQUES
fnac
voyages
P

14.

17. ▶

16.

Palais du Luxembourg, einst für Maria de' Medici erbaut, heute Sitz des französischen Senats.
Palace of Maria de' Medici in the Luxembourg Gardens, now the Senate House.

17.

Blick hinüber zum Panthéon vom Brunnen der Place Edmond Rostand (Boulevard St-Michel).
The Pantheon seen from the fountain in Place Edmond Rostand on the Boulevard St-Michel.

DALLOYAU

15.

18.

18.
Büchertrödler am Ufer der Seine vor dem Louvre.
A bookseller's stall beside the Seine in front of the Louvre.

19./20.
Die Glaspyramide am Eingang des Louvre.
Glass pyramid at the entrance to the Louvre.

CHATELET
PANTHEON
Mairie du Vème

19.

20.

21. ▶

NAPOLEON III EMPEREUR

22.

PALAIS DU LOUVRE
LA PYRAMIDE

21.

Palais du Louvre.

22.

Skulpturen von Maillol im Jardin des Tuileries.
Statues by Maillol in the Tuileries gardens.

23.

Der Königspalast vom Garten aus gesehen.
The Palais Royal seen from its gardens.

24.

Die Kirche St-Germain-des-Prés.
St Germain-des-Prés Church.

25.

Die Place Vendôme, aus einer Ecke des Platzes aufgenommen.
Place Vendôme viewed from one of its corners.

26.

Der kaiserliche Adler von der Triumphsäule auf der Place Vendôme.
The imperial Eagle, detail of the column in the Place Vendôme.

de Flore
la hune
la hune
la hune
Les Deux Ma

FRED

recharge
vehicules
electriques
BNP PARIBAS

CHAUMET
CHAUMET

26.

27.

LE PENSEVR
DE RODIN OFFERT
PAR SOVSCRIPTION
PVBLIQVE AV PEVPLE
DE PARIS MCMVI

27.
Musée Rodin: der «Denker» von Rodin im Museumsgarten; im Hintergrund die Kuppel des Dôme des Invalides.
The statue of «The Thinker» in the garden of the Rodin Museum, with the cupola of the Dôme des Invalides in the background.

28.
Petit Palais und Grand Palais: im Hintergrund die Kuppel des Dôme des Invalides.
The Petit and Grand Palais stretching back to the cupola of the Dôme des Invalides.

30.
Die Pariser Oper genießt Weltruf.
The world-renowned Opera House.

29.
Die Place des Victoires mit dem Reiterstandbild Ludwigs XIV.
Place des Victoires with the equestrian statue of Louis XIV in the centre.

BLANC BLEU
PLEIN SUD
JEANS
HARTFORD

LVDOVICO·DECIMO·QVARTO

ROLEX
COMMER
ACADEMIE NATIONALE DE MUSIQUE

BANQUE BIPOP
BANQUE BIPOP
LIQUOR
Grand Marnier
LIQUOR
MEUNIER BNP PARIBAS
MEUNIER BNP PARIBAS
LANCEL
MATY
MATY
RAYMOND WEIL
PLACE DE CLICHY

31.

31.

Die Kirche Ste-Marie-Madeleine, von der Parisern liebevoll «la Madeleine» genannt.
The Church of St Mary Magdalene, known to all Parisians as «la Madeleine».

32.

Dôme des Invalides.

33.

Vollmond über dem Eiffelturm, aufgenommen von der Passerelle Debilly.
Full moon over the Eiffel Tower from the Debilly walkway.

32.

◀33.
34.

35.36. ▶

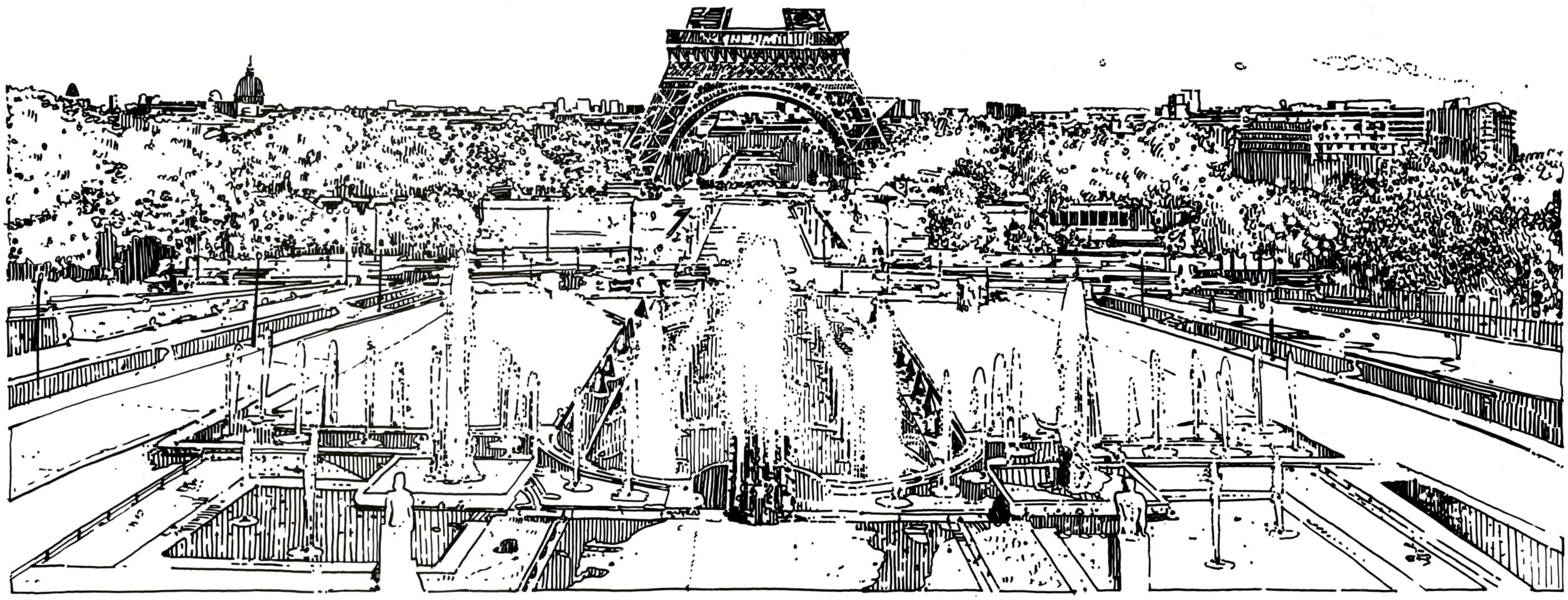

L'HOTEL DES INVALIDES

LE PALAIS DE CHAILLOT

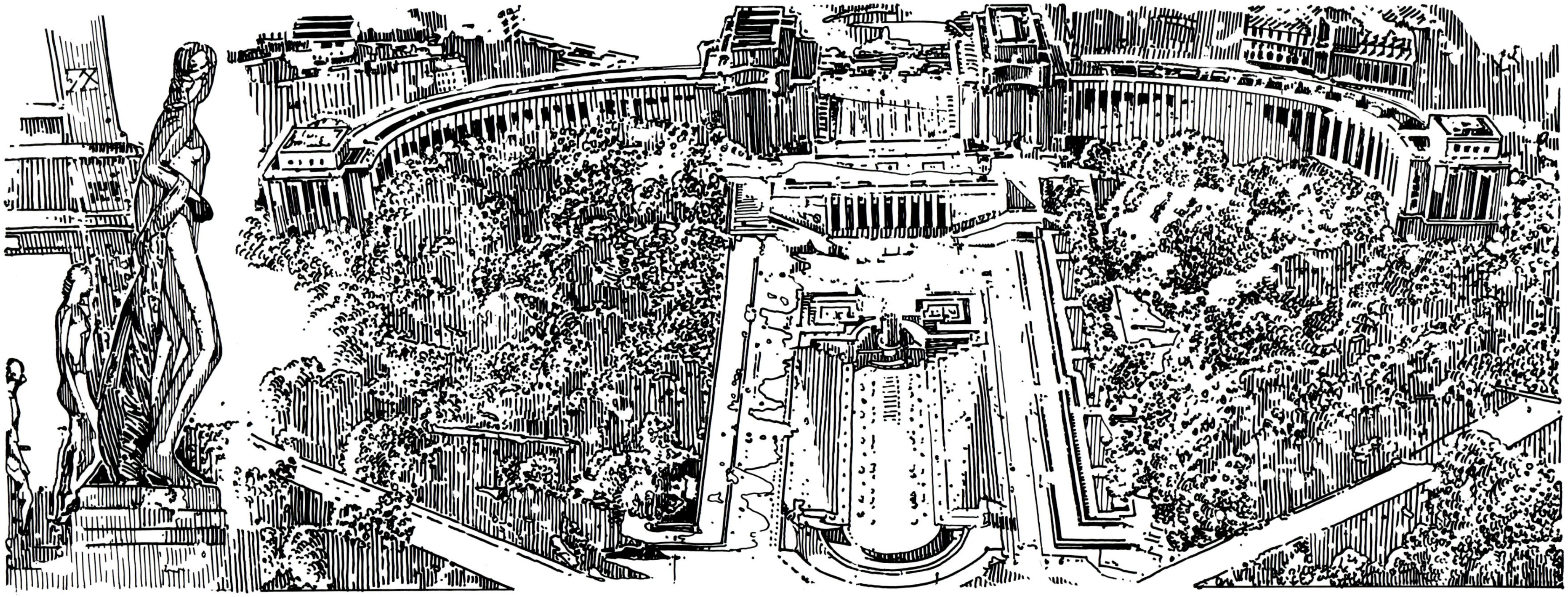

34.

Statuen vor dem rechten Pavillon des Palais Chaillot, gegenüber dem Eiffelturm.
Statues in front of the right-hand pavilion of the Palais Chaillot facing the Eiffel Tower.

35.

Place du Trocadéro, Palais Chaillot, Aussichtsterrasse, Eiffelturm und Champ de Mars.
Panorama of the Place du Trocadéro, Palais Chaillot, the panoramic terrace, Eiffel Tower and Champ de Mars.

36.

360°-Panorama Aufnahme vom Pont Alexandre III.
A 360° panorama around the Pont Alexandre III.

37.

Die Place de la Concorde, vom Jardin des Tuileries aus gesehen.
Place de la Concorde seen from the Tuileries gardens.

38.

Einer der Brunnen auf der Place de la Concorde.
Details of one of the fountains in the Place de la Concorde.

39.

Verkleinerte Kopie der New Yorker Freiheitsstatue über der Seine, gegenüber dem Stadtteil Grenelle.
A small-scale reproduction of the Statue of Liberty on the Seine facing the Grenelle district.

40.

Place de l'Etoile, auf den Arc de Triomphe laufen sternförmig alle Strassen zu.
The Arc de Triomphe in the centre of the immense Place de l'Etoile.

38.

CCF
22h37
CREDIT
AGFACOLOR

PEUGEOT
SHIBA COPIEUR
QUICK ELYS
VERNET

43.

41.

Die Champs Elysées am Abend, von der Kreuzung der Avenue Georges V aus gesehen.
The Champs Elysées by night seen from the Avenue Georges V cross-roads.

42.

Musée de la Gare d'Orsay.

43.
La Défense: die rote Skulptur von Calder.
La Défense: the red sculpture by Calder.

44.
Stadtviertel La Défense: «Les deux Personnages» von Mirò.
La Défense with «Les deux personnages» by Mirò in the foreground.

45.
Abschnitt der Défense vom zentralen Platz aus.
A view of the Défense from the main concourse.

ATLANTIQUE

G.F.F
winterthur
IBM
Crédit du Nord
Midnight Express

46.

7.

MOULIN ROUGE
Féerie
LA NOUVELLE REVUE DU MOULIN ROUGE
DU
MOULIN ROU
Féerie
LES DORISS GIRLS

46./47.
Musée de la Villette und seine Géode.
Musée de la Villette and its Géode.

48.
Das Moulin-Rouge, mit dem Pigalle Zentrum des Pariser Nachtlebens.
The Moulin Rouge, the centre of Paris' night life.

49.
Brunnen im Park von Sacré-Cœur.
Fountain in the Sacré-Cœur park.

50.
Der Square Willette zu Füssen von Sacré-Cœur.
Square Willette at the foot of the Sacré-Cœur.

50.

LE CONSULAT
RESTAURANT LE CONSULAT

CAISSE

12
BOULAN
BOULANGERIE-PATISSERIE
9
J.SUR
AGF
SAUF AUX RIVERAINS
de 15h à 2h
NE
M'ABANDONNEZ PAS

IGERIE
12
ET
RPR
ADHEREZ

53.

LE SACRE COEUR
LE CONSULAT
MONTMARTRE
ROUGE
TABAC
PIGALLE
LA
CRIME

◀54.
55.

51.
Blick auf die zum Montmartre-Hügel führenden malerischen Gassen.
A picturesque view of the alleys leading to the hill of Montmartre.

52.
Die Place du Tertre, das Herz der «Libre Commune de Montmartre».
Place du Tertre: the heart of the «Free Commune of Montmartre».

53.
Maler auf der Place du Tertre.
Artists in the Place du Tertre.

54.
Nachtaufnahme von Montmartre mit Sacré-Cœur.
Montmartre: the Basilica by night.

55.
Montmartre: Moulin de la Galette.
Montmartre: The Galette mill.

56.
Métro-Eingang im Stadtviertel Montmartre.
Entrance to the Métro in the Montmartre district.

METROPOLITAIN
LIGNE № 12
ABBESSES
LIGNE № 12
Musée de Montmartre
12 RUE CORTOT
Tous les jours de 14 h 30 à 17 h 30

56.

Historische und kunstgeschichtliche Recherchen
Historical and artistic research

Hervé Juvin

1.

Attilio Boccazzi-Varotto

Die Tore von Paris schwingen seit langem im Wind, ein endloses Vor und Zurück der Züge, vor allem der regionalen Untergrundbahn Métro, Autoschlangen aus den Vorstädten, die sich durch die Straßen quälen. Die alten Straßen heißen Porte de Saint-Cloud, Porte de Saint-Denis, Porte d'Orléans. Tore, durch die die Menschen von Lutetia, später Paris, Nahrung vom Land erhielten oder von Invasoren bedroht wurden. Tore, an denen Zölle erhoben wurden, an denen man kaufte, verkaufte und Tauschhandel trieb. Tore, die kontrolliert und verteidigt wurden. Tore, die mit ihren Verliesen und Mauern erstürmt wurden. Heute gibt es in Paris praktisch keine alten Mauern mehr. Nur im Marais und in der Montagne Sainte-Geneviève haben ein oder zwei Fragmente der vielen Enceinten die Zeiten überdauert. Diese Umwallungen hatte Paris errichtet und wieder niedergerissen, als es ein Dorf nach dem anderen verschlang. Wo sind eure Weinberge und Felder heute, Auteuil, Bercy und Charonne? Gibt es etwas, das an die Zeit erinnert, als ihr noch keine Stadtteile wart? Die Geschichte Paris' könnte um seine Einfriedungen geschrieben werden: Mauern, Tore, Eisengitter. Schwere, opake Wälle ermüdeten die Pariser rasch. Deshalb griffen sie auf Eisengitter und -tore zurück, die zu den Hauptmerkmalen der Straßen wurden – schmuckloses oder betörendes Gitterwerk. Man findet es an den Fenstern des Palais de la Cité, das heute ein Gefängnis ist, aber auch an Küchenfenstern, um hungrige Passanten davon abzuhalten, den Braten zu stehlen. Tore in öffentlichen Gärten, vergoldete Kreationen in den Höfen der Stadthäuser, verziert mit Lilien und Eichenblättern. Glänzend oder rostig, das Tor ist geöffnet. Lasst uns in Paris eintreten!

The gates of Paris have long swung to the winds from every quarter: an endless back and forth of trains, especially those of the underground and regional Metro, gales of cars blowing in from the suburbs. Porte de Saint-Cloud, Porte de Saint-Denis, Porte d'Orléans - names recalling the ancient roads. Gates through which the people of Lutetia and then Paris could be fed from the countryside or menaced by invaders. Gates for the payment of tolls, for buying and selling, for bartering. Gates to be controlled and defended. Gates to be taken by assault with their gratings, keeps and walls. Today, of course, Paris has lost virtually all its old walls. Almost by chance, indeed, an odd fragment or two has survived at Marais and Montagne Sainte-Geneviève of the series of enceintes the city erected and then tore down as it devoured one village after another. Where are your vineyards and fields now, Auteuil, Bercy, Charonne, does aught recall the time when you were not yet *quartiers*?
The history of Paris could be written around its enclosures: walls, gates, gratings. Heavy, opaque ramparts quickly tired the Parisians and they chose gratings and iron-barred gates as one of the main features of their street furniture. Severe or beguiling gratings. Those in the windows of the Palais de la Cite, now a prison, those of the windows of kitchens to ensure that the roast was not fished out by a hungry passer-by. Gates in public gardens, gilded creations in the courtyards of town houses adorned with fleurs-de-lys and oak leaves. And the gates of the finest palace, bearing the emblems of royalty. Shining or rusty, the gate stands open. Let us enter Paris.

◀ 0 | 90° | 180° | 270° | 315° ▶ 360°

2.

A. B.-V.

Paris erstreckt sich am Horizont, eine lohnenswerte Beute an den Ufern der Seine. Das hungrige Auge sucht und sucht, nur um sich im feinen Straßennetz, in Höfen und an Dächern zu verlieren. Diese „weise" Unordnung, mit der sich Paris schützt, verbirgt jedoch keineswegs seine geheime Geographie, die heimliche Intimität seiner Viertel, Plätze und Märkte, kurzum der Pariser und ihrer kleinen kultivierten Freuden. Wer spricht schon in der Stadt am Fuße des Tour Montparnasse hinter dem Montmartre von den Träumen der Dörfer? Hier ist Paris nur ein Platz, ein riesiger Platz, den bestimmte Formen kennzeichnen. Der Eiffelturm und Notre-Dame. Auf dem Montmartre zur Rechten die Sacré-Cœur, zur Linken die Kuppel des Panthéons und der Tour Montparnasse oder der Turm von Jussieu und die Türme auf der Place d'Italie. So viele Zeichen im weiten Paris, Zeugen der Omnipotenz der Geschichte, der Ordnung, die ihren Weg bestimmt: die religiösen und ökonomischen Zeugen triumphieren, nicht vorhanden sind – seltsamerweise – politische. All diese Zeichen vermögen es jedoch nicht, dem Besucher einen Weg zu skizzieren, noch ihm zu verraten, welchen Weg er einschlagen muss. Es ist besser, die Bilder zu erkennen, die aus der Stadt aufsteigen und ihr Leben einhauchen: Wirtschaftsgebäude und die Métro; Taxis, die an Kreuzungen gestrandet sind, Rendezvous auf den Terrassen der Cafés, Frauen, die auf den Boulevards im Bois flanieren, artige Kinder unter den grünen Bäumen des Parc Monceau, die Treppen, die vom Butte zum Markt in der Rue Lepic führen … Dann fällt einem wieder ein, dass nur ein guter Läufer Paris zu Fuß an einem Nachmittag erkunden kann und dass der Mensch der universale Maßstab ist: sein Schritt, seine Größe, sein Vergnügen. Liegt darin vielleicht das Geheimnis von Paris? Selbst mit ihren Exzessen verteidigt die Stadt ihre Vielfalt, ihren Rhythmus und ihre Landschaften. Sie bringt aus Unstimmigkeiten neue Harmonien hervor mit der Nachsicht, die man erwirbt, wenn man so viele Experimente anstellt.

The horizon comes full circle around Paris, an admirable prey for the taking, abandoned along the banks of the Seine. The right and left banks, indeed, seem but one in this flurry of embankments and gardens, the serried ranks of barges. One's hungry gaze fumbles and rummages, only to lose itself in the fine mesh of streets, courts and roofs, all this sapient disorder through which Paris protects itself, disclosing naught of its secret geography, the furtive, crumpled intimacy of its quarters, squares and marketplaces, of the Parisians, in short, and their little urbane pleasures. Who will speak of their dreams of villages in the town, at the foot of the Tour Montparnasse, behind Montmartre? Here, Paris is space alone, space on the grand scale, where there are certain shapes to serve as landmarks. The Eiffel Tower and Notre-Dame. Montmartre's Sacré-Cœur on its molehill to the right; the dome of the Pantheon and the Tour Montparnasse on the left, or the Jussieu tower and those of the Place d'Italie. All so many signs in the space of Paris, witnesses of the omnipotence of history, of the orders that direct its path: the religious and economic are triumphant, absent, strange to tell, those political. Yet so many signs that have no power to sketch out an itinerary for us, nor point out the road we must take. It is better to espy the pictures that rise from the city, that give it life, in a word: offices and the Metro; taxis aground on crossroads, rendez-vous on the café terraces; the women strolling along the boulevards in the Bois, well-behaved children under the great trees in the Parc Monceau, the stairways that descend from the Butte to the Rue Lepic market. One remembers, then, that to cross Paris on foot is but the task of an afternoon for a good walker, and that man is the universal yardstick: his pace, his size, his pleasure. Is this, perhaps, the secret of Paris? Even from its excesses the city draws a defence of its variety, its rhythm and the nature of its landscapes. It plucks from its discords new harmonies with the indulgence that becomes one whose experiences are so many.

3.

A. B.-V.

Eine Straßenlampe, erschöpfte Touristen – was wäre Paris ohne Notre-Dame, die mit der Selbstsicherheit eines Postkartenmotives über ihrem Vorplatz thront, aber auch mit der Zuversicht derer, deren Augen viel gesehen haben. Vor acht Jahrhunderten folgten Adlige und Bettler, Kleriker und Steinmetze dem Ruf Maurice de Sullys. Sie kamen hierher und errichteten Mauern und Hallen, Bogen und Portale. Leidenschaft und Mysterium waren im Spiel, als die Darstellung der heiligen Szenen das Volk von Paris und Pilger der ganzen Île-de-France an diesen Ort zogen. Die Vorliebe für die Klassik ließ die Schönheit der Gotik langsam in Vergessenheit geraten. Victor Hugo läutete die Renaissance ein. Eugène-Emmanuel Viollet-le-Duc erneuerte, setzte wieder ein und ließ seiner Fantasie freien Lauf. Haussmann ließ die alten Häuser niederreißen, die das Dorf Notre-Dame bildeten. Und das war's oder zumindest beinahe. Acht Jahrhunderte und nur ein Kapitel in der Geschichte von Paris, wie der Besuch der archäologischen Krypta unter dem Vorplatz bestätigt. Meterhohe Erde und Gesteinsschutt, den die Seine angeschwemmt hat, formen das Gewölbe für die Mauerreste, die Zeugnis ablegen von den Barbaren, die hier vor den Königen, vor Rom und vor Paris selbst gelebt haben. Dennoch reichen acht Jahrhunderte aus, um Notre-Dame zu einem glorreichen Zeitzeugen zu machen, der sich nicht mehr greifen lässt. Haussmann ließ die Fläche des Vorplatzes verdreifachen. Dadurch wird man jedoch zum distanzierten Bewunderer eines Monuments. Der Gewinn des Symbols ist der Verlust der Kathedrale. Man muss Notre-Dame nahe stehen, mit der Fassade und den Portalen sprechen. Nur so kann man ihre Botschaft entschlüsseln, ihre Strenge und Bedeutung bis ins kleinste Detail begreifen, ihre Zeichen und Gesten verstehen wie in den Tagen der Gotik, als die Menschen hierher kamen, um das Mysterium von Leben und Tod zu gewahren, das sich innerhalb dieser Mauern offenbarte. Was wäre Notre-Dame, wäre sie nichts weiter als schön?

A street lamp, tired tourists, what would Paris be without her Notre-Dame enthroned on its parvis with the aplomb of a picture postcard, yet also with the assurance of one whose eyes have dwelt on many a different scene? Like the hive of activity eight centuries ago, when nobles and beggars, clerics and masons swarmed to the spot at the call of Maurice de Sully to erect walls and porches, arches and buttresses. The fever of passion and mystery plays, when the representation of sacred scenes drew to the square the folk of Paris and pilgrims from the whole of the Ile-de-France. Then the slow slide into oblivion as a penchant for the classical scorned the beauty of Gothic. A renaissance trumpeted by Victor Hugo. Viollet-le-Duc renewed, reinstalled, and let his own fancy roam. Haussmann tore down the old houses which formed Notre-Dame village. And that was that, or nearly. Eight centuries, but no more than a chapter in the history of Paris as can readily be seen by visiting the archaeological crypt below the parvis, where metres of soil and the debris brought down by the Seine form the roof for the sherds and chunks of walls that are the vestiges of the barbarians who lived here prior to the kings, before Rome, before Paris itself. Yet eight centuries are enough to render Notre-Dame the glorious witness of times beyond our ken. Haussmann has helped us by tripling the area of the square. But this makes us distant admirers of a monument. The symbol's gain is the cathedral's loss. One must rub shoulders with Notre-Dame, chat up its facade and its portals. This alone will unlock its message, restore to every part its strength and importance, its signs and gestures, as in the Gothic days when men came to descry the mystery of life and death revealed in these walls. What would Notre-Dame be were she not more than beautiful?

4.

A. B.-V.

Die Grande Galerie verbindet mit ihrer steinernen Draperie die beiden Türme von Notre-Dame: ein Ehrenplatz für die Premiere der Parisshow! Hinter dem Hôtel Dieu und der Préfecture schafft das alte Palais de la Cité, einst Sitz der Könige von Frankreich und des römischen Kaisers Julian, Platz für den emporstrebenden Kirchturm der Sainte-Chapelle. Die Häuser drängen sich entlang der Straßen aneinander, als ob sie versuchten, einen besseren Blick zu erhaschen. Doch die Raubtiere und mythischen Kreaturen, die Notre-Dame bewachen, wissen genau, dass nichts geschieht, dass niemals etwas geschehen wird, nur die Wolken ziehen am blauen Himmel über den Dächern dahin.

The Grande Galerie links the two towers of Notre-Dame with its stone drapery. A dress circle position for the premiere of the Paris show. Be hind the Hôtel-Dieu and the Préfecture, the old Palais de la Cité, once that of the kings of France and the Roman emperor Julian the Philosopher, provides a chink for the soaring spire of Sainte-Chapelle. The houses huddle tightly together along the embankments, as though to get a better view. Yet the beasts of prey and mythical creatures that guard Notre-Dame well know that nothing is happening, that nothing will ever happen, nothing but the clouds, the wondrous clouds in the sky so blue above the roofs.

0 90° 180° 270° 315° 360°

5.

A. B.-V.

Paris hat seine Vergnügen. Was ist jedoch neben dem reinen Bummeln für die Stadt charakteristisch? Die Pariser haben dieses Vergnügen, das einst als Trödeln bekannt war, zu einer wahren Kunst erhoben. Man bleibt ohne triftigen Grund vor einem Schaufenster oder Zeitungsverkäufer, bei einer Rauferei oder einem Brand stehen. Man nimmt sich Zeit, um zu sehen und zu hören; um das frühe Licht zu genießen, das die Steine der Cité vergoldet; um die Gedanken für einen Moment umherschweifen zu lassen, um der Realität gerade so weit zu entfliehen, dass die eintönige Straße, auf der man schon tausendmal gegangen ist, zu einer ländlichen Gegend wird. So viel Neues, so Vieles zum Entdecken! Innerhalb von Sekunden wird man zum Millionär der Bilder. Pariser und Touristen vermischen sich und genießen die Schönheit der Uferstraßen, der Seine, eines Sommertags. Montaigne bemerkt amüsiert, dass die Pariser aus ihren Häusern strömen, wenn sich der erste schöne Tag ankündigt, nicht willens wegzufahren, gelassen und bereit, an einem Tisch im erstbesten Café Platz zu nehmen. Die Place vor dem Brunnen Saint-Michel mit seiner langweiligen, überladenen Fassade ist an einem solchen Tag schwarz vor Menschen. Die Maigrets des Quai des Orfèvres gegenüber machen es einem schwer, der Versuchung eines kühlen Biers zu widerstehen. Sonnige Uferstraßen erinnern an Seepromenaden. Und dann trifft man noch auf jene, die einfach innehalten, um die ersten Sonnenstrahlen zu genießen.

Paris has its pleasures. Yet which more than sauntering is truly hers? Her inhabitants have elevated this delight, once known as dawdling, to the status of a fine art. To stop for no valid reason, be it shop window or newsvendor, brawl or fire. To take time to see, to listen; to savour the young light gilding the stones of the Cite; to create for a moment the mind warp, the slight break with reality needed to make your hum drum street a countryside, the section trodden a thousand times a promenade. So many new things, so much to discover for the first time. Everyone can be a millionaire rich in pictures, in seconds. Parisians, travellers, tourists mingled in the quality of a time regained, a regard rendered naïf by the sovereign beauty of the embankments, the Seine, a summer's day. Montaigne noted with amusement that when the first fine day comes round the Parisians are all out of doors, loth to depart, easy-going, ready to take a table at the first cafe they find. The square before Fontaine Saint-Michel and its boring facade exuding decor but little water is black with people, you can be sure. It's hard to poke an enquiring finger into the wares on the booksellers' stalls. The Maigrets of the Quai des Orfèvres opposite are hard put to it to resist the temptation of a foaming pint. Sunny embankments seem seaside promenades. And there are those who stop, their appointments forgotten, just to let the light filter through their eyelashes.

0 90° 180°

6.

A. B.-V.

Am Abend taucht das Licht der untergehenden Sonne Paris in ein geheimnisvolles Grau. Das Silbergrau der Seine, das Schiefergrau der Dächer und Straßen, das patinierte, matte Grau der Häuser oder das zarte Grau des kreidehaltigen Gesteins von Notre-Dame und der alten Villen der Île Saint-Louis. Die Ausflugsboote reflektieren im schwachen Licht an den Kaimauern. Zeit, um unter den Bäumen spazieren zu gehen, die das Quai Saint-Michel flankieren. Zeit, die Brücke zu überqueren, die Landluft zu atmen, die von der Île Saint-Louis herüberweht, und die vornehme Zurückhaltung dort zu genießen. Die Buchhändler haben ihre Truhen geschlossen. Notre-Dame trägt das Gewand einer unbekannten Majestät. Die Seine murmelt für die tauben Ohren der Pariser, wetteifert mit dem Stelldichein, der Musik. Die Nacht senkt sich über Paris, die Stadt erwacht.

The setting sun leaves a cloak of grey in its train nearly every evening in Paris. The silver grey of the Seine, the slate grey of the roofs and embankments; the patinated, tired grey of the houses, or the tender grey of the chalky stone of Notre-Dame, the old mansions on Ile Saint-Louis; flashing greys under the tiny suns the pleasure boats are reflecting on the quays. Time to stroll past the trees that line Quai Saint-Michel, whose swaying shadows sculpt the statues anew, or to cross the bridge, breathe the village air emanating from Ile Saint-Louis opposite, and savour its aristocratic reserve. The booksellers have shut their lucky dips, padlocked their chains. Notre-Dame wears the garb of majesty unknown. The Seine murmurs for deaf Parisian ears, vain competitor with assignations, trains to catch, music. Night falls. Paris arises.

◄ 0 | 90° | 180°

7\.

Auf der ehemaligen Place de la Grève kündet das Hôtel de Ville von der Grandeur, dem Reichtum und dem Genie Paris'. Statuen thronen auf ihren Säulen, Fabelwesen auf dem Glockenturm, allegorische Figuren, kein Ornament wurde vergessen. Was verkünden die Herolde, die ihre Trompeten über den Dächern in alle Himmelsrichtungen schwenken, neben dem Ruhm von Paris? Auch wenn das Gebäude sein strahlendes Weiß wiedererlangt hat, und die Architekten, die es in den 70er-Jahren des 19. Jahrhunderts wiederaufbauten, etwas von der Dritten Republik mit der reinen Sprache der Renaissance vermischten, so bergen seine Mauern doch eine lange Geschichte. Den Fängen der städtischen Kaufleute entkommen, dem Missbrauch der Könige und der Kommune während der Französischen Revolution ausgesetzt, war dieser Operettenpalast lange Zeit das Bollwerk der Pariser gegen die Landesregierung. Ein Bollwerk in parisischem Stil, voll Leben und reich verziert, ein Bollwerk, das man leichter über diesen Geist als mit Waffengewalt erobern konnte. Von Etienne Marcel bis zur Zeit Jaques Chiracs war das Hôtel de Ville Symbol für die Unabhängigkeit der Stadt, ihrer Ideen, Sitten und Gebräuche und ihres Lebensstils. 1870, während der letzten Tage der Kommune, als die Armeen von Versailles auf die Stadt vorrückten, entschieden die Kommunarden, das Gebäude in Brand zu stecken, bevor es in die Hand derer fiel, die alles verkörperten – Gewalt, Macht, Frankreich – alles, aber keine Pariser.

On what was once the ancient Place de la Grève, the Hotel de Ville emphatically proclaims the grandeur, the wealth and the genius of Paris. Statues perched on their columns, fabulous beasts on the campanile, allegorical figures, no ornament has been forgotten. And way above the roofs, what else but the renown of Paris is proclaimed to the four winds by the heralds brandishing their trumpets? Even if it has regained its white ardour, if the architects that rebuilt it during the 1870s blended something of the Third Republic into the pure language of the Renaissance, the walls of this edifice are none the less the bearers of a long history. From the slings of the city's merchants directed against the abuses of the kings until the Commune in the 1789 Revolution, this operetta palace was long the rampart of the Parisians against the central government. A rampart in the Paris style, full of spirit and adornment, one that conquered through this spirit rather than by any force of arms. From Etienne Marcel (1316-58) to Jacques Chirac, the Hôtel de Ville has been the symbol of the city's independence, the independence of its ideas, customs and way of life. In the last days of the Commune in 1870, when the armies of Versailles were marching on the city, the Communards preferred to set fire to the building rather than see it fall into the hands of those who were everything – force, power, France – everything, yet not Parisians.

8\.

Hölzerne Pferde, die die Träume der Kinder erhellen. Ungeachtet der Fahrzeugschlange, die sich über die Place de Châtelet und durch die Rue de Rivoli quält, drehen sie sich unablässig auf einem kläglichen Rummelplatz im Kreis, während ihre Reiter so ernst wie Kreuzritter die arrogante Stille des Tour Saint-Jacques respektieren. Die Metzgerszunft machte die Kirche Saint-Jacques de la Boucherie zum Symbol ihrer Macht. Die Kirche wurde jedoch zerstört. Ihren Glockenturm überließ man zunächst Pascal für seine Experimente, dann den Alchimisten für ihre phantasmagorischen Ziele und schließlich wandelte man ihn in eine Munitionsfabrik um. Das Gebäude, ein Zeitgenosse des Hôtels de Ville, widersetzte sich allen Einflüssen der Renaissance. Der träge schlagende Puls der Gotik sucht noch immer hartnäckig das Jahrhundert, dem er angehört, wie jene Pferde, die davon träumen, dem Sieg entgegenzugaloppieren.

Wooden horses that shed a brighter lustre on children's dreams. Heedless of the febrile surge of cars through the Place de Châtelet and the Rue de Rivoli, they turn and turn to the strains of a plaintive fairground organ, while their riders, as serious as any Crusader knight, respect the haughty silence of the Tour Saint-Jacques. The butchers guild had made the church of Saint-Jacques de la Boucherie the symbol of its power. But the church was destroyed, its bell-tower handed over to Pascal for his experiments and the alchemists for their phantasmagoric pursuits before being converted into a munitions factory. A contemporary of the Hôtel de Ville, it set its face against all the Renaissance had to offer. This tardy beat of the Gothic pulse is still stubbornly seeking the century to which it should belong, to construct for itself an impossible erewhon, like these horses, whose infernal round casts a haze of false reality over their dreams of galloping to victory, of heroic charges imbued with all the brutality of war.

9.

A. B.-V.

Das Forum des Halles hat ein ganzes Viertel auf den Kopf gestellt. Die Pavillons Baltard, jene Schirme, die Napoleon III. eingeführt hat, breiten ihre Glasflügel und gusseisernen Kuppeln aus. In den ehemaligen Markthallen von Paris roch es nach dem Schweiß der Portiers, nach dem Blut geschlachteter Tiere, nach Fisch und nach tausenden von Gerüchen, deren Aromen der Muse von Zola und vielen anderen schmeicheln. Heute bietet das unterirdische Einkaufs- und Kinozentrum alles, was das Herz begehrt. Eine dicke Brieftasche richtet hier mehr aus als Muskeln. Dennoch spürt man einen Hauch der alten Magie. Wie einst der Cimetière des Innocents ist das Forum ein Kaleidoskop, dessen veränderliche Muster ein fast vollständiges Phantombild der Pariser liefern. Hier findet man liebenswürdige Schwindler, Bürogehilfinnen, die sich in ihrer Mittagspause auf die Jagd nach einem Schnäppchen machen, Liebhaber von Zusammenkünften jeglicher Art. Das Einzige, was hier interessiert, ist, dem Müßiggang zu frönen. Man schlendert von Schaufenster zu Schaufenster und die Métro bringt jene, die wieder ans Tageslicht möchten, um in der Sonne oder im Schatten der jungen Bäume zu dösen, zurück in die Wirklichkeit.

The Forum des Halles has turned an entire quarter on its head, converted space from up to down. Baltard's pavilions, the umbrellas introduced by Napoleon III, unfurled their wings of glass and their cast-iron vaults skywards, redolent with the sweat of the porters, with the blood of slaughtered animals, with the odour of fish and the thousand and one scents whose bouquet tickled the Muse of Zola and many others besides. The Forum, on the other hand, sinks Lethe-wards in a crater that makes acrophobiacs of the Basilique Saint-Eustache and the old houses nearby, and Charon-like embarks the docile crowds down to the roaring bowels of the Metro. Its works are now those of omnipotent trade, its bouquet that of perfumes à la mode. A place where a thick wallet will move more mountains than thick muscles. Yet a whiff of the old magic remains. Like the Cimetière des Innocents of yore, the Forum is a kaleidoscope whose changing patterns offer a nearly complete identikit of the Parisians: swindlers, office girls on the hunt for a lunch-hour bargain, lovers of encounters of every kind. The one and only concern common to this latter-day vulgus is to stroll in idleness. A piece-by-piece sauntering illuminated by the smile of every shop window. Elsewhere, in that other world of the Forum's gardens, the rumbling Metro provides the bourdon for those who would snooze in the sun, or enjoy the nascent shade of the young trees.

10.

A. B.-V.

11.

A. B.-V.

Tiere oder Maschinen, Tiere und Maschinen – blaue, grüne, gelbe und rostfarbene Fabelwesen toben sich im Brunnen aus. Die menschliche Fantasie und die natürliche Lebensfreude haben eine absurde Manege geschaffen, die einen perfekten Kontrast zu den gotischen Flanken von Saint-Merri bildet. Diese schrecklich präzisen, effektiven und nutzlosen Spielereien, die Tiere und Maschinen, die Nikki de Saint-Phalle und Jean Tinguely geschaffen haben, bewegen spöttisch die Reflexionen des Centre Beaubourg in den Springbrunnen. Maschinen, die demontieren, und Tiere, die wider die Natur sind, zieren das Beaubourg, die Kathedrale der modernen Kunst, mit Wasserspeiern, die jenen ebenbürtig sind, die monströs an den Dachrinnen von Notre-Dame thronen, dem Museum des gotischen Christentums.

Animals or machines, animals and machines, these blue, green, yellow and rust-coloured monsters frolic in La Fontaine. Man's imagination and Nature's *joie de vivre* have struck a common chord, a ring of the absurd. In perfect contrast with the Gothic flanks of Saint-Merri alarmed by this blaze, by these terribly precise, efficacious and useless wheelworks, more insidiously ironic towards the revamped ateliers and the old mansions that wisely stand aloof, the animals and machines devised by Nikki de Saint-Phalle and Jean Tinguely stir the derisory reflections of the Centre Beaubourg in their fountain. Machines that take apart, animals Nature would disown, have endowed the Beaubourg, the cathedral of modern art, with gargoyles on a par with those that monstrously grace the gutters of Notre-Dame, the museum of Gothic Christianity.

◀ 0 | 90° | 180° | 270°

12.

A. B.-V.

Welche Maschinerie veranlasst die Menge vor diesem fremdartigen Schiff mit seinem durchsichtigen Rumpf staunend stehen zu bleiben? Schornsteine und Rohre, das Centre Georges Pompidou verbirgt nichts von dem, was die Anatomie einer künstlichen Maschine ausmacht. Mit Leitungs- und Wasserrohren, mit Rauch und Kabeln, mit Aufzügen und Rolltreppen haben es die Architekten Piano und Rogers geschafft, die Aufmerksamkeit auf dieses lebendige, ungewöhnliche Museum zu lenken. Es gibt keine Ornamente, keine Zugeständnisse. Das Beaubourg macht sich mit einem Lächeln über seine Transparenz lustig. Ebenso wie der Eiffelturm, das Mekka der Besucher, zieht das Centre die Menschenmengen an. Vielleicht, weil sie den vielen Attraktionen und Reizen entfliehen möchten, die die Stadt bietet. Schiff und Fabrik, viel verdankt es seinem industriellen Aussehen. Eine erstaunliche Maschinerie: Es degradiert die meisten anderen modernen Monumente in Paris zu technischen Spielereien, zu reizend, um von Nutzen zu sein. Das Beaubourg räsoniert nicht, es exhibiert. Zum ersten Mal ist der Traum eines Kindes Wirklichkeit geworden, das sein Spielzeug zerlegt, um zu sehen, was im Innern vor sich geht. Das Beaubourg ist ein Museum, das seine Seele an seinen Wänden trägt.

What machinery causes the crowd to form before this strange ship with its see-through hull? Flues and pipework, the Georges Pompidou Centre conceals nothing of that which constitutes the anatomy of an incomparable culture machine. With their pipes and tubes for water, smoke and cables, lift cages and intestinal escalators, its architects Piano and Rogers draw attention to the vital functions of this unusual museum by the use of vivid, glaring colours that confer their elemental force on the mammoth whole. No ornament here, no complaisance. Yet the Beaubourg sports its diaphany with a smile. Neck and neck with the Eiffel Tower as a visitor's Mecca, its multitudes come perhaps to take refuge from the city's host of attractions and enticements. Vessel and factory, it owes much to its industrial appearance: prodigious machinery, it demotes most of Paris's other modern monuments to the status of gadgets too amiable to be of any use. The Beaubourg does not hold forth. It exhibits. It has the strength and the naïvety of a confession, along with its frailty. No matter. For the first time, life has been given to the dream of a child who breaks his toys to see what goes on inside, to a museum that wears its soul on its walls.

13.

A. B.-V.

Wenn man die Rue de Rennes entlangschlendert, nähert man sich dem Tour Montparnasse, der den Himmel zu berühren scheint und seine Anwesenheit in einem Viertel behauptet, das ihm lange Zeit feindselig war. Der höchste Turm Europas wartet mit erstaunlichen Zahlen auf: 210 m, 120 000 t, 7 200 Fenster. Dieser Rekord beeindruckt jedoch die Freunde des Viertels nur wenig, deren Zahl seit der Jahrhundertwende immer größer wird, als die Künstler beschlossen, vom Butte Montmartre zu diesem falschen Parnassos herabzusteigen. Ein falscher Berg, aber ein wahrer Parnassos für Maler, Bildhauer, Schriftsteller und jeden anderen Künstler, egal welcher Herkunft. Etwas von diesem Jahrhundert wurde hier gespielt, zwischen dem »Dôme« und dem »Coupole«, inmitten von Tabak, Alkohol und Jazz. Weshalb sollte der Turm also nicht wie ein Eindringling wirken? Was noch wichtiger ist: Er erhebt sich gewissermaßen in Splendid Isolation über den durchschnittlich hohen Gebäuden, die den Boulevard säumen – eine elegante Methode, um Seinesgleichen unter Seinesgleichen zu lassen und einen einzigartigen Horizont zu genießen: Eiffelturm, La Défense, Montmartre und Front de Seine.

As one moves along the Rue de Rennes, the Tour Montparnasse reaches for the sky and asserts its presence in what was long a hostile quarter. Europe's tallest tower has an impressive array of figures: 210 metres high, 120,000 tons, 7200 windows. A record, however, that cuts little ice with the friends of a quarter whose numbers have never ceased to grow since that day at the turn of the century when the artists decided to descend from the Butte Montmartre to this false Mount Parnassus. Altitudinally a fake, yet the real McCoy for painters, sculptors, writers and artists of every sort and every provenance. Something of our century has been acted out here, between the Dome and the Coupole, against a background of tobacco, drink and jazz. How, then, could the tower not seem a gatecrasher? What is more, it rises in splendid isolation above the average-height dwellings along the boulevard, a polite way of keeping itself to itself and of enjoying a horizon peopled by the Eiffel Tower, La Défense, Montmartre and Le Front de Seine.

14.

A. B.-V.

Gemeinsam mit dem nahen Palais du Luxembourg bietet die Kirche Saint-Sulpice eine theatralische Ansicht *à l'italienne* auf einem Platz, dessen Stille im Widerspruch steht zu den quirligen Hochplätzen am linken Ufer, die nur einen Steinwurf entfernt sind. Liegt es am strengen Blick und dem Predigen der vier Statuen, die den Springbrunnen zieren? Bossuet, Fénelon, Fléchier und Massillon, nur ein episkopales Quartett, residieren im Herzen eines ruhigen, angenehmen Viertels, dessen *bon ton* die provinzielle Patina seiner Höfe und Kopfsteinpflaster zur Geltung bringt. Beinahe zu weiß für das Licht, das Paris gewohnt ist, wirkt die Kirche unwirklich und distanziert. Das, was nicht nach mehr streben sollte als einer ländlichen Pfarrgemeinde, ist mit der Vorliebe für die Klassik in den 30er-Jahren des 17. Jahrhunderts unter diversen Architekten, von Gittard bis Servandoni, zu einem der größten und bekanntesten religiösen Gebäude in Paris aufgestiegen. Im Innern findet man ein herrliches Werk von Delacroix: »La Lutte de Jacob avec l'ange«. Wenn die imposanten Orgeln der Kirche ertönen (die als einzige mit Notre-Dame und Saint-Eustache rivalisieren können), droht der Kampf zwischen Himmel und Erde, Saint-Sulpice mit ihrem Prunk und ihren Statuen in einer Woge erzitternder Steinplatten zu verschlingen.

Along with the nearby Palais du Luxembourg, the church of Saint Sulpice proffers a broad, theatrical façade *à l'italienne* to a square whose calm is out of tune with the swirling high places of the Left Bank a stone's throw away. Is it on account of the stern look and preachings of the four cardinal points, whose statues decorate its fountain? Bossuet, Fenélon, Fléchier and Massillon, no more than an episcopal quartet, reside in the heart of a quiet, well-mannered quarter, its *bon ton* enhanced by the provincial patina of its courts and cobblestones. Almost too white for the light to which Paris is accustomed, the church strikes an unreal, distant note. That which should not have aspired to more than rural parish-hood has risen through the Classical penchant instilled in the 1730s by a bevy of architects, from Gittard to Servadoni, to become one of the biggest religious buildings in Paris, and also one of the most famous. The gilded penumbra that stalks its interior is keenly pierced by Delacroix's Jacob wrestling with the angel. When its great organs (the sole rivals of those in Notre-Dame and Saint Eustache) thunder, the struggle between heaven and earth bids fair to engulf Saint-Sulpice, its pomp and circumstance and its cardinal points amid a welter of wavering slabs.

15.

A. B.-V.

◄ 0 | 90° | 180° | 270°

16.

A. B.-V.

Der Jardin du Luxembourg, für Eingeweihte der »Luco«, ist unbestritten der Lieblingspark der Pariser. Hier finden sie alles, was man für einen unbeschwerten Tag braucht. Es weht ein Hauch ländlicher Idylle, man flaniert, anstatt dahinzueilen, Eltern gehen mit ihren Kindern spazieren, Studenten und Liebespaare genießen die angenehme Atmosphäre. Statuen zieren den Park ebenso wie Teiche, Terrassen und Springbrunnen. Auch das Bizarre findet man hier, Bienenkörbe zum Beispiel, die der städtischen Bienenzuchtschule von Paris gehören. Manch einer kam und kommt auf der Suche nach einem schattigen Plätzchen hierher, darunter Diderot, Baudelaire, Gide und andere ehemalige Stammgäste. Die Anlage erstreckt sich über 20 ha und liegt zwischen einem Palais *à l'italienne,* einem Observatorium und dem Tour Montparnasse. Blumenbeete, saubere Avenuen, Verkaufsstände, der Guignol und eine wahre Statuenflut erinnern daran, dass die Gärten von Paris ein anderes Gesicht der Stadt zeigen. Es sind Orte, an denen Paris vorgibt, jemand anders zu sein. Die ausgedehnten Alleen, die Blumenbeete, Bäume und Rasen voneinander trennen, und die kreisrunden Terrassen, sind eine weitere Möglichkeit alles in Szene zu setzen, ein Kontrast, der veredelt. Nirgends besteht die Gefahr, dass man vom Weg abkommt, dass man Paris vergisst, ungeachtet des Summens der Bienen. So war es jedoch nicht immer. In den Weinbergen, die im Mittelalter die Montagne Sainte-Geneviève bedeckten, thronte einst das Château Vauvert, das sehr begehrt war. Man überließ es den Kartäusern, damit sie den Übeltätern das Handwerk legten, die das Gebiet terrorisierten. Fünf Jahrhunderte residierten sie hier. Sie mussten sogar Maria von Medici gegenübertreten, der florentinischen Gemahlin Heinrichs IV. Sie fand ihren Park zu beengt und sehnte sich nach einer würdigeren Erinnerung an ihre Jugend: eine theatralische Erscheinung, Ornamente in italienischem Stil, im Design jedoch Französisch. Salomon de Brosse schuf das Palais du Luxembourg (um 1616), das heute Sitz des Senats ist. Im 19. Jahrhundert wurde es erweitert, erhielt ein majestätisches Treppenhaus und wurde dekoriert mit Delacroix' Interpretationen der »Göttlichen Komödie«.

The Jardin du Luxembourg, the Luco for those in the know, is indisputably the park dearest to the hearts of the people of Paris. They find therein the ingredients for a slender daily pleasure, so rare everywhere else: an air of the countryside without the countryside itself; promenaders as opposed to scurrying marchers; children taking their mothers for a walk; well-behaved students; lovers to boot and a must; statues of every kind, ponds, terraces, fountains. And even a touch of the bizarre: hives that are the rallying place for the swarms kept by the city's Bee keeping School. Some, perhaps, come in search of shades: those of Diderot, Baudelaire, Gide or other former habitués. Spread over its 20 hectares between a Palace *à l'italienne*, a distant Observatory, an indiscreet Tour Montparnasse, flower-beds, clean avenues, kiosks, the Guignol and a veritable tribe of statues are a reminder that in Paris gardens are but another countenance of the city, a space where it plays at being someone else, at joyful self-deception. The perspectives, the wide walks between the grove and the circular terraces are just another way of setting the stage, a contrast that enriches. Need this be a cause for surprise? Nowhere is there any risk of losing one's way, of forgetting Paris, despite the humming of the bees. It was not always thus. Over the vineyards that clothed on the approaches to Montagne Sainte Geneviève in the Middle Ages there once stood Château Vauvert, haunted, of course. It was left to the Carthusians to rid the area of gangs of evildoers. During the five centuries of their residence, they even had to stand up to Maria de' Medici, the Florentine wife of Henry IV, who found her park too hemmed in and yearned for a more worthy reminder of the palazzi of her youth. A theatrical appearance, ornaments in the Italian style, but thoroughly French in design, the Palais du Luxembourg that today's senators enjoy was the work of Salomon de Brosse (circa 1616). Enlarged in the 19th century, it was endowed with a majestic staircase and decorated with Delacroix's interpretations of the Divine Comedy.

◀ 0 | 90° | 180° | 270° | 315° ▶ 360°

17.

Enrico Formica

Ein runder Platz wie dieser Springbrunnen, dessen Sprudel sich wie die Streben eines Fächers ausbreiten. Abseits des geschäftigen Treibens am Boulevard Saint-Michel bieten die drallen Rundungen des Panthéons eine angemessene runde Antwort. Soufflot kreierte die Kombination einer Kuppel über einer Säulentrommel, die auf der Fassade eines griechischen Tempels ruht. Der Baumeister starb an gebrochenem Herzen, als er mitansehen musste, dass die Mauern unter dem Gewicht der Kuppel Risse bekamen. Das Panthéon begann als Kirche, die Sainte-Geneviève, der Stadtheiligen, geweiht war. Zur Zeit der Revolution wurde sie zum Tempel der Republik und ab diesem Zeitpunkt zur letzten Ruhestätte führender Persönlichkeiten, von denen einige nur ein kurzes Gastspiel gaben wie zum Beispiel Mirabeau und Marat. Vom Platz oder vom Boulevard aus betrachtet, hat das Panthéon zwischen all den Geschäften und Zeitungsständen nichts Feierliches an sich, geschweige denn etwas, das an ein Grabmal erinnert. Im Innern findet der Besucher jedoch ein wahres Grab, beeindruckend und eisig; ein Mausoleum, in dem die großen Männer der Republik, Gelehrte, Künstler und Politiker, auf die Unsterblichkeit der Erinnerung hoffen. Merkwürdig scheint, dass Frankreich nur eine Frau, Sophie Berthelot, in die Reihen der Großen aufgenommen hat. Der Besucher würde zweifellos über die überladenen Fresken lächeln, wäre da nicht das schwermütige Geplapper des Fremdenführers ... Und er denkt sicher daran, dass ihn draußen ein herrlicher Tag auf den Terrassen des Jardin du Luxembourg erwartet.

A round square, like this fountain, whose jets spread out to form the ribs of a fan. Set apart from the bustle of the Boulevard Saint-Michel, the plump curves of the Pantheon offer a fittingly rotund response. This combination of a dome stretched over a drum resting on the façade of a Greek temple was designed by Soufflot, who died of a broken heart when he saw its walls begin to crack on the weight of the dome. It began life as a church dedicated to the city's patron saint, Sainte Geneviève, only to become a temple of the Republic at the time of the Revolution, and hence the resting-place of the leading figures of the day, though the tenancy of some, such as Mirabeau and Marat, was exceedingly brief. There's not much solemnity, let alone a funeral note, about the Pantheon when viewed from the square or the boulevard in the company of shops and newspaper stands. Inside, however, the visitor will find a veritable tomb, a gelid, immense mausoleum wherein the Republic's great men, savants, artists, politicians, implore the passing tribute of a sigh. Odd, perhaps, that France has only judged one woman, Sophie Berthelot, fit to share this gloom and the heroic glow that spreads over frescoes so grandiloquent that those who come to admire would willingly remain to smile, were it not for the lugubrious patter of the cicerone. And to think that it's such a splendid day outside on the terraces of the Luco!

18.

A. B.-V.

19.

A. B.-V.

20.

A. B.-V.

21.

A. B.-V.

In Secondhandbuchläden stöbern, in der Hoffnung eine seltene Ausgabe oder eine alte Postkarte zu ergattern – nichts könnte weiter von der Strenge des Louvre entfernt sein. Dennoch war der Ursprung dieses stolzen Palastes eine Bibliothek. Eine königliche Bibliothek, die der Invasion endloser Bestseller entging und herrliche Manuskripte, Stiche und Gemälde barg, die sie zu einem embryonalen Museum machten. Zu den wenigen Konstanten im Leben des Louvre gehört seine beinahe magisch wirkende Anziehungskraft auf Kunstwerke. Hier befand sich die Grande Galerie der Könige. Als die Herrscher ihre Residenz nach Versailles verlegten, öffnete der Louvre seine Pforten für Maler, Bildhauer und Musiker. Die Revolution machte ihn zu ihrem ersten Museum und das Kaiserreich erweiterte ihn, um Platz für die Schätze zu schaffen, die man in ganz Europa erbeutet hatte – viele sind bis heute nicht in ihre Heimat zurückgekehrt. Alles war vorbereitet, um den Louvre zu einem der wenigen Universalmuseen der Welt zu machen, obwohl seit dem Ende des 19. Jahrhunderts der Ferne Osten zur Provinz des Museums Guimet wurde. Auf einer Strecke von mehreren Kilometern durchlebt man fünf Jahrtausende Geschichte und entdeckt die Unendlichkeit menschlicher Träume. 1989 wurde im Louvrehof als neuer zentraler Eingang die Glaspyramide des Architekten I. M. Pei eröffnet.

To browse among the wares of the second-hand booksellers in the hope of unearthing a rare edition, an old picture postcard, a photo of the belles of the Naughty Nineties – nothing, it would seem, could be further from the austerity of the Louvre. Yet a library was the *fons et origo* of this proud palace. A royal library, it is true, spared from the invasion of our interminable string of best sellers, replete with richly illuminated MSS, engravings and paintings that made it a museum in embryo. One of the rare constants in the life of the Louvre, indeed, has been its power to attract, as if by magic, works of art. The kings had their Grand Gallery here, and when they moved to Versailles its slats opened to admit a swarm of painters, sculptors and musicians. The Revolution chose it as the home of its first Museum, the First Empire enlarged it to provide room for treasures looted throughout the length and breadth of Europe, many of which have never returned to their rightful homes. The stage was thus set for the Louvre to become one of the world's few universal museums, though since the end of the 19th century the Far East has become the province of the Guimet. A few kilometres offer a route across five millenia and many times around the world in the discovery of the infinity of human dreams. Antiquity, too, is recalled by the pyramid installed in the Cour Napoléon in 1989 by the American architect Ieoh Ming Pei as a revolutionary way of dealing with the problems raised both by the growing number of visitors and the decrepitude of the place.

22.

A. B.-V.

Akte waren Aristide Maillols Stärke. Seine drei Grazien beleben die ordentlichen Blumenbeete und die geraden Wege in den Tuileriengärten mit einer angemessenen Dosis Sinnlichkeit. Sie haben die Augen niedergeschlagen, nicht jedoch vor der millionsten neugierigen Kamera, sondern in wehmütiger Sehnsucht nach ihrer wahren Heimat unter dem blauen mediterranen Himmel.

Nudes, not frigid prudes were the forte of Aristide Maillol (1861-1944), and these Three Graces confer a refreshing dose of robust sensuality on the oh, so neat flower-beds and the oh, so straight walks of the Jardin des Tuileries. Yet their eyes are downcast. Not, we may be sure, before the millionth prying lens, but in wistful longing for their true home under the blue Mediterranean sky.

◀ 0 | 90° | 180° | 270° | 315° ▶ 360°

23.

A. B.-V.

Bescheidenheit, allerdings auf eine Art, die man kaum bestätigen würde, sollte die Ambition des Herzogs von Richelieu verbergen, als er die Kardinalswürde erhielt und sich daran machte, ein Palais für sich erbauen zu lassen, das sich rasch zu einem Königspalast entwickelte. In den Augen seiner Zeitgenossen erinnerte die Place allerdings mehr an ein Palais als an einen Palast. Am Treffpunkt der legendären Liebschaften des Regenten, wurden unter der Ägide der Herzöge von Orléans Jahrmärkte abgehalten und Kirchweihen gefeiert. In den Gebäudeflügeln, die drei Seiten des Parks umschlossen, waren Boutiquen und über drei Etagen Wohnungen untergebracht, während im Park selbst Einkaufspassagen mit Waren und Zerstreuung jeder Art lockten. Liebeleien mit dem schönen Geschlecht in den Galeries de Bois führten die Rangliste der Vergnügungen an. 1780 erschien der offizielle »Guide des Filles du Palais Royal«, in dem man fremden Besuchern erklärte, wer was machte und für wie viel. Casanova eilte hierher, um den Pulsschlag von Paris zu fühlen, wann immer er sich in der Stadt aufhielt. Diderot promenierte hier mit »meinen Gedanken, die meine Dirnen sind«. Nach Waterloo verspielte Blücher seinen hart erkämpften Lohn. Die moralisierende Mentalität der Mittelschicht des 19. Jahrhunderts säuberte den verruchten Ort und versetzten die Gärten des Palastes in Lethargie, unerreichbar für den erweckenden Kuss, bevorzugter Ort für Tauben, alternde Helden des Staatsrats, Kinder, Pensionäre und ein paar abblätternde Statuen.

Modesty of a kind, albeit hardly one that we would acknowledge, was sought to cloak his vaulting ambition by the Duke de Richelieu when he received his cardinal's hat and set out to build for himself a Palais Cardinal that soon rose to Royal by devise. Yet it was not long before the place savoured more of a palais than a palace in the eyes of its contemporaries. A trysting place for the legendary amours of the Regent (those rollicking suppers in the small apartments that now house our Council of State!), it hosted fairs and kermises under the aegis of the cash-strapped dukes of Orléans. Wings thrown up on three sides of the park were occupied by boutiques and three storeys of flats, while in the park itself shopping arcades dispensed merchandise and every sort of pastime. Dalliance with the fair sex in La Gallerie de Bois headed the list of such sports, and a very official «Guide des Filles du Palais Royal» appeared in 1780 to provide the passing stranger with an idea of who did what and for how much. Casanova hurried here to feel the pulse of Paris every time he was in town. Diderot promenaded with those «whores, my thoughts». After Waterloo, Blücher gambled away the fruits of his pillaging, rough justice indeed. The moralising middle class mentality of the later 19th century, however, bowdlerised the place in a spate of Gallic Comstockery, condemning the gardens of the Palace to a lethargy beyond the reach of any wakening kiss, sans every thing apart from pigeons, elderly worthies of the Council of State, lovers of decorations and old china, children, pensioners heliotropically shifting their metal chairs, and a few flaking statues.

◀ 0 | 90° | 180°

24.

E. F.

Saint-Germain-des-Prés ist zwar ein großer Platz in Paris, aber einer mit nur wenig Symbolen: ein befremdlicher Kampanile mit Portal, eine Kirche von bescheidenen Ausmaßen, verglichen mit den weltlichen Gebäuden in ihrer Nachbarschaft, Straßen, von denen man nicht weiß, ob sie tatsächlich zu dem Platz gehören, eine Apotheke und Caféterrassen. Diese Merkmale des mittelmäßigen Paris' nehmen Gestalt an, sobald der Name Saint-Germain-des-Prés fällt. Was bisher als leerer, gesichtsloser und reizloser Raum erschien, wird zu grellen Bildern, vor denen jegliche Vagheit flieht: Boris Vian und seine Trompete, das »Rose Rouge« und das »Tabou«; Sartre, Juliette Gréco und der Existentialismus; Basementjazz und die »Intellektuellen«; die parisische Ausgabe, ihre großen Themen, ihre berühmten Stimmen. Das Zentrum des linken Ufers befindet sich hier. Wer verschwendet unter den feurigen Fresken eines piekfeinen Salons schon einen Gedanken an das Grab eines polnischen Königs in der Kirche Saint-Germain-des-Prés? Oder an die Abtei, die einst von diesem Turm aus ein Gebiet kontrollierte, das so groß war wie die gesamte Île-de-France? Oder an jene wie Verlaine, Maurras und Péguy, die den Ort zum Treffpunkt der nationalen Literaten machten? Ein Platz der Freiluftcafés, Treffpunkt der Jugend und der nicht mehr ganz so Jungen auf der Suche wonach? Das Wunder von Saint-Germain-des-Prés liegt wohl in seinem schwach ausgeprägten Bezug zur Wirklichkeit.

Saint-Germain-des-Prés, such a large square for Paris, yet short on symbols. A strange campanile-cum-porch, a church of modest proportions compared with the embonpoint of its lay neighbours, streets uncertain whether they really belong to the square that strike off whether they list, a drugstore, cafe terraces. These ingredients of run-of-the-mill Paris however, soar in the imagination once the name Saint-Germain-des-Prés is pronounced. What seemed till now an empty, featureless and unappealing space overflows with strident images before which all vagueness flies: Boris Vian and his trumpet, the Rose Rouge and the Tabou; Sartre, Juliette Greco and existentialism; basement jazz and the «intellectuals»; Parisian publishing, its great causes, its famous voices in the wilderness. The Left Bank, in a word, has its quintessence here. Who spares a thought for the tomb of a king of Poland at Saint-Germain-des-Prés under the fiery frescoes of some swish salon? Or for the abbey which, from this tower, once controlled a domain as extensive as the Ile-de-France itself? Or for those such as Verlaine, Maurras and Peguy, who made this the rendez-vous of the nation's literati, their *bêtes noires* their effectual fires? An awning decorated with pleasing Chinese characters, or on a field vert, outdoor cafés, a tree or two, a host of the young and not-so-young in search of what? The miracle of Saint-Germain-des-Prés lies in its having accoutred its legend with so little, its carving out of such a sturdy existence in spite – or should one say because? – of its tenuous links with reality.

◀ 0 | 90° | 180°

25.

E. F.

Wie die Place des Vosges, aber mit offensichtlicherer Feierlichkeit, wie die Place des Victoires, jedoch in all ihrer Pracht unversehrt, ist auch die Place Vendôme (einst Place Louis-le-Grand) ein königlicher Platz. Der Platz ist dazu geschaffen, die würdige Bühne für eine Königsstatue zu bilden, die die Blicke auf sich zieht, postiert im Zentrum eines in sich geschlossenen Raums, umgeben von schmucklosen Gebäuden, reine Requisiten, die nur dazu dienen, die Aufmerksamkeit auf das einzig würdige Objekt zu lenken. Die Bronzesäule hat eine bewegte Geschichte durchlebt. Während des Aufstands der Kommune wurde sie gestürzt, möglicherweise unter Anstiftung des Malers Courbet. Heute ist der Besucher mehr von der Harmonie der umliegenden Gebäude beeindruckt, einer Harmonie, die dem Architekten Hardouin-Mansart zu verdanken ist: Risalite, Rustika, Arkaden, korinthische Pilaster, Mansarddächer. Die nachfolgenden Regierungen erlebten die wahren Fürsten der Gegenwart: Banker, Finanziers und multinationale Konzerne protzen mit einem kosmopolitischen Luxus, der sich in die nahe gelegenen Straßen ausbreitet. Das Schimmern von Perlen, ein glitzernder Diamant, das Rascheln von Seide und Nerz, eine Limousine, die vorübergleitet, das beneidenswerte Selbstbewusstsein jener, für die ein Taxi stets zur rechten Zeit zur Stelle ist. Die Place Vendôme, Heimat des »Ritz« und der Juweliere, hat sich in ein Schmuckkästchen mit internationalem Gepränge verwandelt.

Like the Place des Vosges, but with a fuller dose of naked solemnity, like the Place des Victoires, though with all its pride intact, the Place Vendôme (formerly Place Louis-le-Grand) is another royal square, a square where all is designed to provide a worthy stage for the statue of a king, the centre and focal point of every gaze, to be set in the middle of a closed space, attended by buildings innocent of ornament, mere props enhancing the only object worthy of attention. The Place Vendôme may be said to have achieved this ideal better than any other, even though the new king's part fell to history's first Little Corporal, whose statue was placed on a column that proved the downfall of the painter Courbet (see photo 26). Today, one's admiration – a sign of the times – is more readily showered on the harmony of the buildings around, a harmony that springs from the symmetry the architect has skilfully employed to create a rhythm through the simple arrangement of triangular fronts and truncated corners, and the superb flow of his pillars and attic windows. The ensuing reigns have witnessed in shrouded, well-guarded secrecy the true princes of the day, bankers, financiers and multinational company men, sport a cosmopolitan luxury that has spilled out into the streets nearby. A gleam of pearls, a sparkling diamond, the rustle of silk and mink, a Rolls gliding by, the maddening self-assurance of those for whom a taxi will always materialise at just the right moment. Home of jewellers and the Ritz, Place Vendôme has become just a casket lined with international ostentation.

26.

A. B.-V.

An allen vier Ecken des Säulensockels wacht ein Adler, Symbol für Napoleons kurzlebiges Kaiserreich, über die Place Vendôme, ohne dem Fries, der sich im Hintergrund an der Säule entlangzieht, Aufmerksamkeit zu schenken. 1806 ließ Napoleon das ursprüngliche Reiterstandbild Ludwigs XIV. durch eine Bronzesäule der Grande Armée ersetzen, in Erinnerung an den Sieg bei Austerlitz. Die Säule wurde aus eroberten russischen und österreichischen Kanonen nach dem Vorbild der Trajanssäule in Rom gegossen. Am 16. März 1871 stürzte man sie als Symbol des imperialen Despotismus im Zuge des Kommune-Aufstands, vermutlich auf Veranlassung des Malers Courbet. Nach dem Scheitern des Aufstands, wurde Courbet dazu verurteilt, die Kosten der Wiederaufrichtung zu tragen – sein Ruin. Seine Werke wurden unter Wert verkauft und er ging in die Schweiz ins Exil. Dort starb er auch. Der Künstler, der mit seinem Pavillon »Le Realisme« einer ganzen Stilrichtung ihren Namen gab, war bisher das einzige Opfer der kriegerischen Kaisersäule.

An eagle, symbol of Napoleon's short-lived empire, casts a haughty eye on Place Vendôme from each of the four corners of the pedestal of its column, heedless of the warlike scenes that spiral upwards behind. The equestrian statue of Louis XIV inaugurated here in 1699 was replaced in 1810 by the Grande Armée Column, modelled on that of Trajan in Rome, and made from the bronze of 1200 cannons captured after the battle of Austerlitz (1805). On the 16th of March 1871, it was pulled down as a symbol of imperial despotism by the Communards at the instigation of the realist painter Gustave Courbet. A great crowd gathered to watch the ceremony. Little good did it do Courbet, however. When Paris was regained a few days later by the forces of Thiers, temporarily installed at Versailles, he was ordered to foot the bill for putting the column to rights. The works in his atelier were sold and he spent a period in prison before being exiled to Switzerland, where he died. The artist who gave us «Les Semeuses» has so far been the only victim of this bellicose imperial column!

27.

A. B.-V.

»Le Penseur« wendet dem Dôme des Invalides den Rücken zu. Rodins Fragment der Humanität, sein verstörter Geist, heimgesucht von Zweifeln und Ängsten, und dieser Koloss sind miteinander verflochten wie eine ruhige Flamme. Worüber könnten sich diese beiden führenden Charaktere der parisischen Bühne unterhalten haben? Zwei Jahrhunderte trennen sie, mehrere Revolutionen, zwei Imperien und unzählige gegensätzliche Bilder, die im Kopf Rodins kreisten, für den das Grand Siècle ein Mysterium gewesen sein muss. Die Vorgaben der Perspektive, die diese eindrucksvolle Kombination beherrschen, stehen symbolisch für die Größe Paris'. Einige wenige Striche aus der Feder des Geographen skizzieren eine Stadt, deren Geschichte und menschliches Genie ihr zuweilen die Größe eines Kontinents verleihen.

The thinker turns his back on the Dôme des Invalides. Rodin's fragment of humanity, his troubled mind assailed by saucy doubts and fears, and this colossus twisted like a silent flame. The serenity of great classical art, and this very rare balance between the technical capabilities of a period and an architect's need to express himself. What words could be exchanged between these two leading characters on the Parisian stage? Two centuries apart, together with a string of revolutions, a couple of empires and a host of contrasting images in the thoughts of Rodin, for whom Le Grand Siècle would have been a mystery. The dictates of perspective that govern this striking combination are symbolic of the size of Paris itself. A few short strokes of the geographer's pen encircle a city which history and human genius have on occasion swelled out to the ambit of a continent.

28.

A. B.-V.

Mit Betonung glasgefasster Arkaden, aber auch mit einem Gespür für den Dekor sind das Petit Palais und das Grand Palais seit beinahe einhundert Jahren unter dem arroganten Blick des Dôme des Invalides in einen wortlosen Dialog verstrickt. Ein stiller Dialog, erfüllt von Nostalgie und dem Verlangen nach einem neuen Jahrhundert, die Belle Époque, als Paris zum letzten Mal von sich selbst als Zentrum Europas träumen konnte, als Hauptstadt der Welt. Der Pomp und der Lebensstil, die Festivals, die Torheiten dieser Jahre reflektiert die Architektur der beiden Palais, die sich einreihen in die weltlichen Kathedralen des Industriezeitalters, des Zeitalters von Eisen und Stahl, berühmt durch Orsay und Saint-Lazare, die Bahnhöfe im Osten und Norden, und andere Zeugen entlang der Rue Réaumur. 1900, zur Zeit der Weltausstellung in Paris, forderte der Triumph der Industrie die Vermählung von Eisen und Glas mit Stein. Das Augenmerk richtete sich auf Strukturen, Treppen und Glasverkleidungen. Das monumentale Portal des Petit Palais, die riesige 43 m hohe Glasgallerie und das herrliche Treppenhaus des Grand Palais sind überschwängliche Meisterwerke, die ein Eigenleben führen. Die beiden Paläste, die so anders sind als die anderen, strahlen ein Gefühl der Lebensfreude und des Glücks aus.

With emphasis, yet with a clear sense of decoration, of glass-enclosed arcades, the Petit Palais and the Grand Palais have for nigh on a hundred years been engaged in a wordless dialogue under the haughty gaze of Les Invalides. A silent dialogue imbued with nostalgia, a yearning for the turn of the century, La Belle Époque, when for the last time Paris could dream of itself as the centre of Europe, the capital of the world. The pomp and circumstance, the festivals, the follies of these years are reflected in the architecture of these two Palais, which must be ranked with those lay cathedrals of the industrial age, the age of iron and steel, known as the Orsay, Saint-Lazare, East and North railway stations, the covered markets and other demonstration edifices along Rue Réaumur, especially their splendour. On the occasion of the 1900 Universal Exposition, the triumph of industry demanded the marriage of iron and glass with stone, hence the importance accorded to structure, stairways, glass panellings. The monumental porch of the Petit Palais, the immense glass gallery 43 metres high, and the fine staircase of the Grand Palais are exuberant masterpieces in their own right. A feeling of joie de vivre, of happiness, almost, yet a happiness that does not shrink before facile effects, emanates from these palaces so different from the rest.

29.

E.F.

Vor welchem Anblick bäumt sich das Pferd auf, das Ludwig XIV. mit einer Hand bändigt? Vielleicht versucht es dem erniedrigenden Schicksal seines Vorgängers zu entkommen, dessen Bronze 1792 eingeschmolzen wurde, um daraus das heutige Werk zu formen. Die Place des Victoires, der Platz, den einst der Duke de la Feuillade seinem Souverän darbot – wobei er sich selbst ruinierte –, hat viele Gründe, sich über städtische Revolutionen zu beklagen. Jene, die auf Haussmann folgten, rissen die herrlichen Villen nieder, die 1883 verhinderten, dass man in die Rue Etienne-Marcel gelangte. Damit war der Platz seiner Harmonie beraubt, die er der Hand Hardouin-Mansarts verdankte, der die Villen um die Statue in einheitlichem Stil kreiert hatte. Nahe dem Palais Royal, der Galerie Colbert, dem Zentrum der Fertigkleidungsbranche, in dem die neuen Häuser errichtet wurden, bleibt die Place des Victoires ein schönes Beispiel für die städtische Ordnung, die die königlichen Plätze dem Paris des 17. und 18. Jahrhunderts aufdrängten.

At the centre of the circle of elegant women, of mannequins and their favourite creators, towards which flashing view is this horse rearing, held in check by Louis XIV with one hand? Perhaps it is seeking to flee the degrading destiny of its predecessor, whose bronze was melted down in 1792 to be replaced by the present work. The Place des Victoires, the square offered to his sovereign by the original Duke de la Feuillade, who ruined himself in the process, had much to reason to complain about urban revolutions. Those who came after Haussmann demolished those of the fine mansions that prevented the opening the Rue Etienne-Marcel in 1883. The square was thus shorn of the harmony it had received at the hands of Hardouin-Mansart (1646-1708), who designed its strictly similar mansions all around the central statue. Close to the Palais-Royal, the Galerie Colbert, centre of the designer styled ready-to-wear trade, where the new fashion houses have taken up residence, the Place des Victoires remains a fine example of the «new urban» order the royal squares imposed on 17th and 18th-century Paris.

30.

E. F.

Meisterhaft oder pompös, ein Medley aller europäischen Stile, Vorläufer eines wahren Empirestils – die Pariser Oper wurde in jeder Hinsicht kritisch beurteilt. Als *Opus majus* des Zweiten Kaiserreichs, das unterging, bevor das Werk vollendet war, und als Meisterstück des jungen Architekten Charles Garnier ist die Oper mehr als nur eine Bühne. Sie ist selbst ein Spektakel, eine Melange aus Musik, Malerei und Rhetorik. Musen und Genies greifen in die Saiten der Lyren und künden bis unter den Giebel von der Grandeur lyrischer Kunst. Die Zeit ließ die Farben verblassen, die Garniers Palette entsprungen sind, als er seine farbigen Steine und Marmore, seine vergoldeten Statuen und seine Ornamente aus Bronze und Kupfer großzügig über das Gebäude verteilte. Das Treppenhaus, das Foyer de la Danse und die Prunkzimmer sind jedoch gut erhalten. Der Balettfreund tut gut daran, sich dem Luxus dieses Vergnügens hinzugeben und zu vergessen, dass die Oper einen Platz beherrscht, der zwar als seine Dienerin geschaffen wurde, gleichzeitig jedoch Ort des Bigbusiness, des Handels und der Banken ist, jener anderen Welt, für die Haussmann die Grands Boulevards und die Avenue de l'Opéra zerstörte, damit Arbeit und Vergnügen sich wie lustige Kumpanen auf der imperialen Bühne fühlen konnten.

Masterly or pompous, a medley of every European style, progenitor of a genuine Empire style, the Paris Opéra has received the full gamut of critical assessment. *Opus major* of a Second Empire that did not last long enough to see it completed, masterpiece of a young graduate in architecture, Charles Garnier (1825-98), the Opéra is something more than a place for shows. It is itself a spectacle, a mélange of music, painting and oratory. Muses and winged genii brandishing lyres proclaim the grandeur of lyric art right up to the gable. Time has sternly washed out some of the hues that sprang from Garnier's rainbow palette as he sprinkled his coloured stones and marbles, gilded statues and ornaments in bronze and copper over the building with a lavish hand. The great stairway, the Foyer de la Danse and the state apartments, however, have conserved their fires. The balletomane will do well to let himself sink into the pleasure of luxury trumpeted abroad as in a manifesto, and forget that the Opéra reigns over a square that was indeed designed as its handmaid, but is also the haunt of big business, trade, banks, that other world for which Haussmann hacked out the Grands Boulevards and the Avenue de l'Opéra so that work and pleasure could feel boon companions on the festive imperial stage.

◀ 0 | 90° | 180°

31.

A. B.-V.

La Madeleine, die Kirche im Stil eines griechischen Tempels, erhebt sich am Zusammenfluss der Grands Boulevards, dem Viertel des Showbusiness, mit der geschäftigen Rue Royal als Pendant zum Palais-Bourbon unweit der Place de la Concorde auf der anderen Seite der Seine. Das Gotteshaus ist der heiligen Maria Magdalena geweiht. Der feierlich klassische Mantel, der den Namen dieser reuigen Sünderin umhüllt, dient vielleicht dazu, das Bühnen- und Nachtvolk zu verführen, für das feierlicher Ernst eine notwendige Zierde ist, um erfolgreich zu sein. La Madeleine hat viele Begräbniszeremonien erlebt, von der Bestattung des korsischen Königs Carbone bis zu jener von Thierry Le Luron. Ganz Paris hat sich im Halbdunkel in ihre Bänke gequetscht, denn ihr Baumeister Vignon hielt am griechischen Modell fest, das keine Seitenbeleuchtung erlaubt; und das Licht von Paris entspricht bei weitem nicht jenem der Akropolis. Napoleon widmete diesen Tempel seiner Grande Armée und die Mysterien von Paris haben die Kirche zum irreligiösesten Gotteshaus gemacht, dessen Fassade noch nie ein Kreuz geziert hat, aber auch zum parisischsten.

The Greek temple church erected at the confluence of Les Grands Boulevards, the showbiz district, with the business-clad Rue Royale as a pendant to the Palais-Bourbon some way off beyond the Place de la Concorde on the other side of the Seine is known as La Madeleine, since it is dedicated to Mary Magdalene. The somewhat severe classical cloak wrapped around the name of this repentant sinner serves, perhaps, to seduce the stage and nocturnal folk, for whom solemnity is a necessary adornment to flourish in the face of life and death. A string of funerals from that of Carbone, a Corsican known as the king of the Pigalle, to that of a mimic, Thierry Le Luron, have huddled all Paris, and Paris as a whole, along its pews in semi-darkness, since the stern respect for Athens displayed by its architects forbade illumination from the side, and it need hardly be said that the light of Paris cannot hold a candle to that of the Acropolis. Napoleon associated La Madeleine with his Grande Armée, and the mysteries of Paris have conspired to make it both the least religious of all no cross has ever graced its façade – and one of the most Parisian of all – the city's churches.

49.

A. B.-V.

Dieser pausbäckige Junge wächst offensichtlich mit Vergnügen heran. Er könnte das Symbol für den Butte sein, wo Enthaltsamkeit und Maß keine Bedeutung haben. Nahe dem Mont des Martyrs, auf dem der heilige Denis gesehen worden sein soll, der seinen Kopf unter dem Arm trug, standen einst Mühlen neben Schänken, in denen säuerlicher Wein von minderwertiger Qualität freigebig serviert wurde. Die enorme harntreibende Wirkung des Weins ist in einem populären Sprichwort verewigt: »Da gibt es einen Wein in Montmartre, von dem trinkst du eine Pine und pinkelst ein Quart.« Nur ein Weinstock hat entlang der Rue des Saules überlebt und zur Zeit der Weinlese bietet sich die Gelegenheit zu einer großen Zeremonie. Die Müller waren nicht die einzigen, die ihre Ärmel hochkrempeln mussten. In einem Bericht aus der Zeit Ludwigs XV. findet man eine Beschwerde über die Verwüstungen, die Soldaten und andere freche Individuen auf Weizen- und Roggenfeldern angerichtet haben. Die guten Zeiten von Montmartre begannen 1780 mit der Errichtung der Enceinte Les Fermiers Généraux. Mit dieser Mauer wurde auch eine Steuer auf alle Weine eingeführt, die in einem bestimmten Bezirk verkauft wurden, zu dem der Butte nicht gehörte. Eingefleischte Trinker entflohen dieser schrecklichen Umwallung, um ihren Durst zu stillen, ohne ihr Portmonee zu sehr zu beanspruchen. Die Mauer hielt dem Wachstum der Stadt nicht stand, doch der Brauch, sich in Montmartre einen zu genehmigen, hat sich gehalten und wird wie alle guten Traditionen noch heute gepflegt. Zu den Exponaten im Montmartre-Museum gehört unter anderem die Einrichtung eines Bistros, dessen einziger Gast vielleicht Utrilllo war.

This chubby lad rising with evident pleasure and an abundance of life could be the symbol of the Butte, where abstinence and sobriety have always been virtues *non gratae*. Beside the Mont des Martyrs, where St Denis is said to have been seen with his head tucked underneath his arm, mills once stood cheek by jowl with taverns where a sharpish wine of no great quality was served with a generous hand. Its prodigious diuretic efficacy has been immortalised in a popular saying: «Montmartre wine is the flowing sort/You drink a pint, and out comes a quart». One solitary vineyard has survived along the Rue des Saules, and its vintage time is the occasion of great ceremony. Yet the millers were not the only ones to lift their elbows high. A report from the days of Louis XV complains of the damage caused by soldiers and other ribald individuals in the fields of wheat and rye. Montmartre's good times began later in 1780 with the building of the Les Fermiers Generaux wall. This wall, which, «by immuring Paris, made Paris murmur», was accompanied by the introduction of a tax on all wines sold within a certain precinct that did not include the Butte. Hardened drinkers naturally fled outside this abominable enceinte to quench their thirst without overdraining their wallets. The wall, of course, did not survive the city's outward throes, but the custom of slipping up to Montmartre for a quick one had taken hold, and, like all good traditions, had come to stay. A rightful repayment, perhaps, can be seen in the fact that the Montmartre Museum is probably the only one to have the furniture of a bistro among its collections, the very bistro which, even had Utrillo been its only customer, would have possessed enough to clinch its reputation.

◀ 0 | 90°

50.

A. B.-V.

Als Symbol eines wohlwollenden, gnädigen Gottes blickt die Sacré-Cœur herab auf die Schornsteinaufsätze der Großeltern, mit ausgebreiteten Armen, als wolle sie die ganze Welt mit ihrem Mantel umhüllen, jedoch mit einem blutenden Herzen, das in ihrer göttlichen Brust gut zu erkennen ist. Vielleicht hofft die krypto-byzantinische Basilika Paris als Ganzes bedecken zu können. Ihr Architekt, Paul Abadie, der die Kathedrale Périgueux wiederhergestellt hat, konzentrierte sich vollkommen darauf, das Bauwerk grandios, imposant, ja vernichtend zu gestalten, ebenso, wie die Provinzler aus Versailles vor nicht allzu langer Zeit die Kommune vernichtet hatten. Sorge bereiteten ihm jedoch die Tunnel und Schächte, das Gewicht der Kuppeln und das 95 m hohe Minarett. Die Arbeiten begannen 1876 und dauerten bis 1919, als die Pariser von unten bewundernd zur Basilika emporblicken konnten. Doch wie wunderbar ist der Blick von der Sacré-Cœur auf Paris! Man braucht nur die Menschen zu fragen, die sich hier an sonnigen Tagen aufhalten. Zuschauer und Spektakel, die Kirche strahlt über Paris und badet in seinem Licht. Es ist schwer zu sagen, wer von den beiden dem anderen was verdankt.

Symbol of a benevolent, pardonful God, the Sacré-Cœur looked down on the chimney-pots of our grandparents, its arms outstretched to embrace the world at large within its mantle, yet with its bleeding heart well evident in its divine breast. Perhaps this crypto-byzantine basilica hopes to cover Paris as a whole. Its architect, Paul Abadie, who restored Périgueux Cathedral, directed all his talents to making it grandiose, imposing, even crushing, just as the provincials from Versailles had crushed the Commune not long before. Headaches, however, were everywhere in store in the form of tunnels and shafts, and the weight of the cupolas and the 95-metre minaret was not the least of his worries. Work began in 1876 and went on until 1919, when at last Paris could look up at the basilica in astonishment. Yet how fine does Paris herself appear when seen from the Sacré-Cœur! Ask the crowds that flock up here on fine days. The basilica acquires its just measure in this reciprocal seeing and being seen. Onlooker and spectacle, it shines upon Paris and bathes in her light. Hard, indeed, would it be to say what each owes to the other.

◀ 0 | 90° | 180°

51.

A. B.-V.

Graffiti und Postkarten, Restaurants und Kabaretts. So abgedroschen diese Klischees auch sind, sie charakterisieren den Montmartre und machen seinen Charme aus. Nach dem Anblick der Monumente, die Haussmanns militärischem Geist entsprungen sind, nach dem Lärm und dem Gedränge und einer Überdosis an Sehenswürdigkeiten ist es erholsam, Montmartre zu besuchen und die Allée des Brouillards entlangzuschlendern, zwischen den Gärten, in denen Gérard de Nerval spazieren ging. Hier gibt es kein Muss, keine Museen, nur kleine niedrige Häuser, gewundene Straßen, einen Weinberg, schattige Wege und betagte Treppen, die in die Rue Lepic führen. Vorsicht ist geboten! Die Steine sind lose und die Geländer von Rost zerfressen. Hier kann sich Paris gehen lassen, hier muss es sich nicht treu sein. Häuser und Gärten sind die Wohnstätten von Künstlern, Malern, Sängern und Musikern, von Literaten und Theatervolk, die ihre Umgebung eifersüchtig verteidigen. Vor allem aber findet Paris mit Montmartre einen verborgenen Teil seines Gedächtnisses wieder und erinnert sich an jene Tage, in denen es selbst ein Dorf war und keine Hochhäuser seinen Himmel verdunkelten.

Graffiti and postcards, nosheries and cabarets. These most commonplace features of the village of Montmartre are also the source of its charm. After a stomachful of monuments, of the severe enfilades shot through Paris by Baron Haussmann's military-minded ideas of urban renewal, a bellyful of noise and hustle, an overdose of views of this, that and the other, how restful it is to mount Montmartre, to skirt the Allée des Brouillards between the gardens where Gérard de Nerval was wont to stroll. No musts, no museums here, just small, low houses, winding streets, a vineyard, shaded walks and aged stairways down to Rue Lepic. Watch out, however! Those stones have worn loose, that railing has its full complement of rust. Here Paris can forget herself, to herself be no longer true. Method there is, none the less, in this apparent madness. Low houses ride on the ghosts of quarries whose gougings have for ever debarred the rearing of heavy mansions in hewn stone. Houses and gardens that are the haunts of artists, painters, singers, musicians, adpersons, literary and theatre folk whose life-frame is the subject of jealous and effectual care. Above all, Montmartre nurtures a secret plot in the city's memory, brushes aside our century and reminds her of the days when she was herself a village, and no lofty buildings darkened her sky.

52.

A. B.-V.

Die Place du Tertre ist das Forum des Dorfes, das Montmartre von alters her ist. Der Morgen ist erfüllt vom Duft frischen Brotes oder heißen Kaffees mit einem Schuss Alkohol, der einen aufwärmt. Die hölzernen Rollladen werden spät hochgezogen, verschlafen grüßen sich die Nachtmenschen, die endlich in die Stadt gehen, um den Rest des Tages zu verbringen. Paris ist unnahbar. Taxifahrer lenken ihre Fahrzeuge nur ungern über diese mit Kopfsteinpflaster versehenen Straßen. Die Métro verlässt ihre Tunnel und verwandelt sich in eine Drahtseilbahn. Anatole, der Wächter der »Libre Commune de Montmartre«, patrouilliert mit seinem Stab und seinem Dreispitz auf den Terrassen. Zur Zeit der Jahrhundertwende entschied eine Gruppe böhmischer Burschen, dass es für Montmartre an der Zeit sei, sich von Frankreich zu lösen, von einem Paris, das weniger parisisch als universell war, eines das in den Farben gemalt werden kann, die die Fantasie am stärksten ansprechen.

Place Tertre, the forum of the village that Montmartre has always been. Its morning air is laden with the scent of fresh bread, or hot coffee laced with a finger of raw alcohol to warm the cockles, or so it seems. Wooden shutters open late to allow the exchange of the sleepy salutations of night people who will eventually go downtown to wear out the rest of the day. Paris, indeed, is remote. Taxi-drivers are loth to put their vehicles through the mill on these cobbled streets. The Metro leaves its tunnel to become a funicular. Anatole, Warden of the Free Commune of Montmartre, patrols the terraces with his great staff and cocked hat. Since that day at the turn of the century when a group of merry bohemian lads decided it was time for Montmartre to secede from France, the Place du Tertre has symbolised the omphalos of picturesque Montmartre, of a Paris less Parisian than universal, one that can be painted in the colours that best please your imagination's eye.

46.

A. B.-V.

47.

A. B.-V.

Stadt in der Stadt, Palast der Techniken. Das Géode fängt die Lichter von Paris ein, die Grande Halle kündet vom Triumph des Stahlzeitalters, Kunst und Industrie sind am Ende doch vereint. La Villette, eine neue Stadt, erbaut von einem Schwarm Architekten auf 55 ha inmitten von Kanälen, Schiffen und verlassenen Fabriken und Lagerhäusern, in einem vergessenen Viertel (wer hätte gewusst, dass Paris ein 19. Arrondissement hatte?). Ein vielgestaltiger Platz, dessen einziger gemeinsamer Nenner die Technik ist. Die Technik der Zukunft im Géode, jene von gestern und heute in der Stadt der Wissenschaft und Industrie. Ein Echo der Architektur des 19. Jahrhunderts in Mérindols großem Fleischmarkt, heute die Bühne für Ausstellungen und Shows. In den letzten zehn Jahren hat sich La Villette immer weiter vergrößert. Es ist zu einem überraschenden Beispiel für das neue Paris geworden, das in der nord-östlichen Ecke der Stadt langsam erwachsen wurde.

City within the city palace of the thousand and one techniques. The Géode beckons all the lights of Paris, the Grande Halle proclaims the triumph of the age of steel, art and industry reconciled at last. La Villette, a new town built of knowledge and culture on 55 hectares amid a wilderness of canals, barges and abandoned factories and warehouses in a forgotten district (hands up all those who realised Paris had a 19th arrondissement) by a bevy of architects. A multiform space whose only common denominator is technics. Those of the future in the Géode's hemispherical cinema, those of today and yesterday in the City of Science and Industry. An echo of the 19th-century architecture in Mérindol's great meat market, now the scene of exhibitions and shows. The steady expansion of La Villette over the last ten years has made it a surprising illustration of a new Paris that has been slowly coming of age in the city's north-east corner.

48.

E. F.

Der Boulevard de Clichy zwischen Blanche und Pigalle ist der Ort, an dem Paris die Nacht ausklingen lässt. Noch machen die Neonschilder Reklame, noch quälen die flammenden Segel des »Moulin Rouge« den Himmel. Stripperinnen und Cancantänzerinnen haben die Maske der Heiterkeit abgelegt und interessieren sich nur noch für eine letzte Tasse Kaffee im kalten Licht der Morgendämmerung. Das alte Räuber- und Gendarmspiel wird hier noch immer gespielt, wenngleich sich die unscheinbaren und unbekannten, zu zart besaiteten Kriminellen, die die Seiten von Pierre Mac Orlan und Francis Carco füllen, heute lukrativeren Geschäften widmen. Die Türsteher der Nachklubs verabschieden die letzten Hostessen, die ihr Singledasein wieder aufnehmen, nachdem der unwirsche Kunde gegangen ist, der ihnen vorgerechnet hat, dass Champagner billiger sein sollte als Gold. Die Türen diskreter Hotels öffnen sich für die Paare, die aus glitzernden Limousinen steigen, eingehüllt in eine Wolke aus Musik, Parfüm und Zigarettenrauch. Die Lebensmittelhändler, die die ganze Nacht geöffnet haben, zählen ihre Einnahmen. In Kürze werden die ersten Straßenreiniger kommen, um die Überreste der Nacht in die Gullys zu fegen. Ein Betrunkener schnarcht mit offenem Mund inmitten der Place Pigalle. Blanche und Pigalle verkörpern die andere Seite des Lebens, die andere Seite von Paris.

The Boulevard de Clichy between Blanche and Pigalle is the place where Paris comes to an end at the birth of each new day. The neon signs still blare their messages, the flaming sails of the Moulin Rouge still crucify the sky. Strippers and cancan *figurantes*, their erstwhile lovely nudity now demurely concealed, have thrown off their mask of brightness, their only concern a last cup of coffee in the cold light of dawn. The old game of cops and robbers is still played out there in the shadows, though the wan and none too tender criminals who thronged the pages of Pierre Mac Orlan and Francis Carco have graduated from run-of-the-mill misdeeds to more lucrative traffickings. The doormen of the night clubs bid farewell to the last hostesses, their singleness regained, long after easing out that disgruntled customer who reckoned champagne ought to cost less than gold. Yet at what price should one's fancy roam when pleasure never is at home? The doors of unquestioning hotels open to admit hurrying couples that spill out of glitzy limos in a swirl of music, perfume and cigar smoke. The all-night grocers start to tot up their takings. In a while, the first squads of cleaners will sweep the jetsam of the night into the gutters. A drunkard snores through gaping jaws in the very middle of Place Pigalle, his head against the curb of its unheeding fountain. Blanche and Pigalle, part of life's seamier side, of the other side of Paris.

43.

A. B.-V.

Die andere Dimension von Paris. Mit einem Blick lässt sich nicht alles erfassen. Zu hoch, zu breit, zu weit. Vergleiche drängen sich auf: Baumstämme, Wälder. Weshalb jedoch sollte jemand daran liegen, die Künstlichkeit von La Défense durch die Natur zu verbergen? Kunst ist List und deshalb Affektiertheit, Technik, Anstrengung und Architektur. La Défense bedroht die künstlerischen Leinwände von Paris nicht, reduziert jedoch vieles mit der elementaren Strenge seiner primitiven Formen und mit dem Verzicht auf Verzierungen auf ein malerisches Postkartenmotiv. Vielleicht ist La Défense einfach die kapriziöseste der Stadtschönheiten, die vergänglichste, jene, die am wenigsten verführt …

The other dimension of Paris. A glance is not enough to take everything in. Too high, too wide, too far, space itself is engulfed. Similes, of course, come to mind: tree trunks, forests. Yet why should one wish to deny the artificiality of La Defense through a resort to nature? Art is artifice, and hence affectation, technique, labour and architecture. La Defense does not threaten the artistic canvas of Paris, but bids fair to reduce much of it to the picturesque of a postcard through the elemental strength of its crude shapes, its refusal of ornamentation. May it not simply be that La Defense is the most capricious of the city's beauties, the most volatile, the least enticing?

45.

A. B.-V.

Zwei Alphabete der Formen schmiegen sich aneinander und nehmen sich gegenseitig aufs Korn. Ein Wechselspiel der Würfel überall am Horizont von Paris, dem die fragwürdige Ehre des Unvollendeten zuteil wird. La Défense materialisiert ein Ideal, das als Modernität bekannt ist, ein Ideal, das die Stadt besser in ihre Außenbezirke verbannt hätte, das anzieht und gleichzeitig abstößt. Das Geschäfts- und Einkaufsviertel könnte das starke Gegenmittel vertragen, das Mirós solide Kunst enthält. Diese Figuren vor dem aufgeblähten Segel des Palais des Congrès künden von einer Naivität, die an die Hochhäuser erinnert, das riesige geometrische Ganze, in dem Paris nach einer Zukunft sucht.

Two alphabets of shapes jestingly rub shoulders to seek each other out. An interplay of cubes forgotten on all the horizons of Paris, which gains a slight sense of the unaccomplished. La Defense materialises an ideal known as modernity that the city would rather have relegated to its exurbia, an ideal that its abundant space both beckons and repels. This business and shopping centre needed the robust antidote provided by Miro's solid chunks of art. These figures before the bellying sail of the Palais des Congrès tell of a naïvety which reveals that of the tower blocks, of the immense geometrical whole wherein Paris looks for a future, though without believing over much, praise be, in her chances of becoming another Manhattan.

◀ 0 | 90° | 180° | 270° | 315° ▶ 360°

44.

A. B.-V.

◀ 0 | 90° | 180° | 270° | 315°

41.

A. B.-V.

Die Uhr des CCF zeigt 22:37 Uhr an. Die hellen Lichter des Champs-Élysées erleuchten Terrassen und Arkaden. Wird La Marseillaise (Spitzname für das Relief von Rude am Arc de Triomphe) wieder einmal bereit sein, weiteren Kriegen aus dem Weg zu gehen? Bei »Fouquet's« trifft man sich, um zu sehen und gesehen zu werden – frische Spieler für ein Spiel, das man hier bereits im 19. Jahrhundert gespielt hat, in den Tagen des Kommens und Gehens zwischen dem Zentrum und dem Bois, als die Schönen und ihre Liebhaber prüfende Blicke von einem offenen Wagen in den anderen warfen. Musset, Beau Brummel, La Belle Otero und Liane de Pougy, Stammgäste an den kultivierten Tischen des »Chez Maxim« und des Foyers der Oper, eure Avenue de la Reine ist begraben unter einer traurig banalen Straße, die Banken, Büros, Arkaden, Boutiquen und Schaufenster säumen, der billige Glanz multinationaler Konzerne, der weder schick ist noch schockiert. »Les Champs« – ein Provinztraum, der in Paris vom Weg abgekommen ist.

The clock of the CCF has stopped for good at 22.37. The bright lights of the Champs-Elysées beam down on promises *à la carte*, terraces and arcades. Will La Marseillaise (the nickname of the mammoth Depart des volontaires de 1792 alto-relievo added by Rude to the Arc de Triomphe) be once again content to steer clear of other wars? At Fouquet's, those who wish to be seen quiz each other, fresh players in a game that was already on the go here in the 19th century, in the days of trips to and fro between the centre and the Bois, where belles and their lovers gravely cast scrutinising stares from one open carriage to the next. Musset, Beau Brummel, La Belle Otero, Liane de Pougy, habitués at the refined tables at Chez Maxim and the foyer of the Opéra, your Avenue de la Reine lies buried under a sadly banal mile of banks, company offices, arcades, boutiques and showrooms, its menu naught but the price-listed dreams of cinemas and restaurants, the cheap splendours churned out by the multinationals, neither chic nor shocking. «Les Champs», a provincial dream that has lost its way in Paris.

42.

A. B.-V.

Heute schnaufen keine Züge mehr im Gare d'Orsay, wenngleich die Menschen noch immer in Scharen kommen, um eine Reise auf den Schienen der Kunst oder der Erinnerung zu unternehmen. Das riesige Bahnhofsgebäude am linken Ufer vor den Tuileriengärten hat den Charme eines Palastes, dem Handel und der Industrie geweiht, jenen neuen Majestäten, die die Eisenbahn verkörperte. Dennoch ist es ein Trompe-l'Œil-Palast, denn selbst 1898 schämte sich der Architekt Laloux noch für das verwendete Metall und verhüllte das eiserne Gerüst mit gemeißelten Frontispizen, Pfeilern und gigantischen Statuen. Der Gare d'Orsay ist ein Porträt der Mixtur aus Kühnheit und Naivität, Archaismus und Erfindungsgabe, die die Zeit zwischen 1848 und 1914 kennzeichnet, jene Jahre, als Paris die Hauptstadt des europäischen Festlands war, eine Brücke zwischen der alten Welt, die in der Geschichte verhaftet war, und der neuen, die sich am Horizont abzeichnete. Das Musée d'Orsay ist weniger ein Museum als ein Lagerhaus für die Souvenirs der jüngsten Vergangenheit: die ersten Fotos, Tanzcafés, die Tanzlokale des Montmartre, die Erinnerung an eine neu gewonnene Freiheit, Formen und Farben, Zutaten für ein beinahe abgeschlossenes Jahrhundert. Auf drei Ebenen überwindet das Musée d'Orsay die Grenzen zwischen den Künsten und stellt die gesamte Bandbreite eines Lebensstils zur Schau. Die Impressionisten haben einen Ehrenplatz, vor allem in den Sälen mit Oberlicht. Sie befinden sich in Begleitung der Stadtplaner von Paris, der Presse, der Oper des Zweiten Kaiserreichs, des lebenslustigen Paris' der Belle Époque, der Plakatmaler und der Fotografen. Orsay, die Reise in die Vergangenheit, bezieht seine seltsame Strenge aus einem konstanten Wechselspiel zwischen dem, was bereits Geschichte ist, und dem, was noch immer Teil des Lebens ist, vielleicht Kindheitserinnerungen, Erinnerungen der Großmutter oder die vergilbten Seiten in Sammel- und Familienalben.

No trains now huff and puff from the Gare d'Orsay, though travellers still come in droves to embark on a trip along the rails of art or memory. An enormous edifice anchored to the embankments of the Left Bank in front of the Jardins des Tuileries, the Gare has the charms of a palace, one devoted to trade and industry, the new majesties that symbolised the railway. A trompe-l'œil palace, none the less, since its architect Laloux felt ashamed of his use of metal, even in 1898, and draped his iron framework with a riot of sculptured frontons, pillars and gigantic statues. A fair portrait, this, of the mixture of audacity and naïvety, archaism and inventiveness that marked the period 1848-1914, the sixty-odd years when Paris was the capital of the Continent, a bridge of decades between an old world resting on the pages of history and our new version just below the horizon. Despite its title, the Musée d'Orsay (1986), is not so much a museum as the storehouse of the frail souvenirs of our recent past: the first photos, the *caf' conc'* music halls and Montmartre dance halls, the memory of new freedoms won, shapes, colours, the quickening pace, the many ingredients of this near ly completed century. Laid out on three levels, the Orsay sets aside the traditional frontiers between the arts to display the full thickness of a way of life, of thought and of feeling. The Impressionists have pride of place, especially in the rooms with overhead lighting, but in the company of Paris's town-planners, the Press, the Opéra of the Second Empire, the gay Paris of the Belle Epoque, the poster artists and photographers. Orsay, our memory lane. This not-quite-a-museum draws its strange strength from a constant interplay between that which is already labelled as history, anonymous, objective, and what is still part of our inner being, whether as childhood memories, granny's recollections or the yellowing pages of scrapbooks and family albums.

ist besser, ein weitläufiger, Schwindel erregender Platz, den eine Stadt formt, die sich offenbar selbst den Rücken zukehrt und auf allen Seiten in Ungewissheit verkriecht. Paris hat sich versteckt. Nur die Tore und Terrassen der Tuilerien und die Zwillingsvillen des Architekten Gabriel erinnern daran, dass es auch noch eine Stadt gibt. Überall sucht das Auge nach Fixpunkten: der Obelisk aus Luxor, der Eiffelturm, die Glaswände des Grand Palais, die die Vegetation überragen, die sich öffnet, damit man den Champs-Élysées bewundern kann. Der erfahrenere Blick wird in der Ferne den Dôme des Invalides, die Hôtels des Quai d'Orsay und das Palais Bourbon ausmachen. Gabriel hat es verstanden, Monumente, Statuen, Springbrunnen, Bäume und Rasen in Einklang zu bringen. Die Place de la Concorde verleiht der Stadt einen Newlook, ein Synonym für Paris, das Schulen, Bräuchen und Konventionen nichts zu verdanken hat. Der 35 m hohe ägyptische Monolith blickt auf die Statuen der Städte Frankreichs, auf Springbrunnen mit pausbäckigen Putten, Nereiden und Delphinen und auf neugierige Touristen – eine vielgestaltige Entourage.

be better, wide open, dizzy space formed by a city that seems to turn its back upon itself and slink away in uncertainty on all sides. Paris in hiding, with only the gates and terraces of the Tuileries, and the twin mansions Jacques Gabriel (1698-1782) added to his square, to remind one that there's a town out there. Elsewhere the eye roams in search of signs and points of reference: the Eiffel Tower rides herd on the obelisk from Luxor; the glass walls of the Grand Palais rise above a screen of vegetation that opens to admit the Champs-Elysées. The more knowledgeable gaze will pick out the Dôme des Invalides, the Quai d'Orsay buildings and Palais Bourbon in the distance. Gabriel's skill lay in welding monuments, statues, fountains, nature, trees and lawns into a sagely balanced whole. La Concorde, indeed, is something of a new look for a city, a synonym for Paris that owes nothing to schools, modes, conventions. Statues of the towns of France, fountains with chubby putti, Nereids and dolphins, and eager tourists form a heterogeneous entourage upon which the 35-metre high Egyptian monolith can look down with the sublime indifference that four millenia of contemplating man and his works most amply justify.

39.

A. B.-V.

Wem sagt der Name Jeanne-Emilie Baheux etwas? Vermutlich niemandem, obwohl jeder ihr Bild kennt. Sie war die kleine Hutmacherin aus Nancy, die dem Bildhauer Frédéric-Auguste Bartholdi als Modell diente für die Statue »der Freiheit, die die Welt erleuchtet« in Paris und New York. Die Brücke, die die Allée des Cygnes überspannt, ist in Sternenbanner gehüllt, die der Neuen Welt huldigen. Die Hochhäuser der Skyline von Paris reichen jedoch nicht annähernd an die Wolkenkratzer von New York heran.

For whom does the name Jeanne-Emilie Baheux ring a bell? Nobody, to be sure, though her image is known to one and all. She was the little milliner from Nancy that Auguste Bartholdi chose to hold high the torch of liberty, both in Paris and New York. The bridge straddling the Ile des Cygnes is draped in stars and stripes to better honour the New World, while the skyline of Paris itself now bristles with high-rise buildings with a faint resemblance to New York's veritable skyscrapers.

◄ 0 | 90° | 180°

40.

A. B.-V.

Der Arc de Triomphe überragt die Bäume um ein Vielfaches, die die Place Charles-de-Gaulle (früher Place de l'Étoile) umrahmen. Er steht an einer Via Sacra der letzten Tage, die am Louvre und den Tuileriengärten beginnt und sich über die Place de la Concorde und entlang der Avenue des Champs-Élysées erstreckt. Der Bogen, der heute eine Mischung verschiedener Regierungen und Stile widerspiegelt, verdankt seinen Ursprung (1806) Napoleon, der ein Monument zu Ehren seiner Armeen schaffen wollte. Die Vollendung des Werks überließ man der Restauration, die darauf jedoch keinen wirklichen Anspruch erhob. 1836 weihte Louis Philippe den Bogen ein, der 20 Jahre Zielscheibe des Gespötts von Paris war. Am Ende verstummte das Gelächter jedoch vor dem feierlichen Ernst, der die Träume eines Volkes verkörperte, und vor dem Grab seines Unbekannten Soldaten.

The Arc de Triomphe rears high above the ring of trees encircling the Place de l'Etoile (renamed Charles de Gaulle in 1970). It stands at the head of a latter-day Via Sacra that starts from the Louvre and the Jardin des Tuileries and continues through the Place de la Concorde and along the Avenue des Champs-Elysées to spill past the grandeur of this single arch a noisy legion of featureless buses and cars. A hotchpotch of regimes and as many styles, the arch owes its origin in 1806 to Napoleon, who wanted a monument to glorify his armies: a giant elephant, perhaps. It was an arch, however, that was chosen, and it was left to the Restoration to slothfully terminate a work to which it had no honest claim. Inaugurated during the reign of Louis-Philippe in 1836, the Arc was the laughing-stock of Paris for twenty years. In the end, however, gales of laughter were stilled by the serene solemnity becoming to a nation's dreams, and the natural resting-place of its Unknown Warrior.

◀ 0 | 90° | 180° | 270° | 315° ▶ 360°

35.

A. B.-V.

Von der Place du Trocadéro und dem Palais de Chaillot genießt man einen herrlichen Blick auf den Eiffelturm, eine Perspektive, die die Herzen von Fotografen und Touristen höher schlagen lässt. Im Zuge der Weltausstellung 1937 wurde das Palais an einem Ort errichtet, den bereits Napoleon als Place für seinen Sohn, den König von Rom, in Erwägung gezogen hatte. Symbolträchtige Statuen blicken finster auf geschickte Skateboarder und Inlineskater. Die Inschriften in goldenen Lettern an den Giebelseiten stammen von Paul Valéry. Hauptanziehungspunkt ist jedoch die zentrale Terrasse, die auf den Eiffelturm blickt. Durch die Bäume der Gärten erspäht man den Tour Montparnasse und den Dôme des Invalides. Zur Rechten sind einige Hochhäuser des 15. Arrondissements zu erkennen. Die Seine ist zwar sehr nah, aber nicht zu sehen. Die Bühne beherrscht der Eiffelturm am Ende des symmetrischen Champ de Mars, der die lange, niedrige Silhouette der Ecole Militaire akzentuiert, die das Bild komplettiert.

From the Place Trocadéro and the Palais Chaillot, Paris once again spreads out in broad perspectives to the joy of photographers and the relief of rubbernecking visitors. It was the 1937 Universal Exposition that produced the Palais where Napoleon had contemplated the erection of a place for his son, the king of Rome. An art déco affair, it unfurls its curved wings around terraces, ponds and fountains. Its pot-pourri comprises adept skate-boarders and roller skaters, symbolic statues sternly frowning at the passer-by, maxims by Paul Valéry engraved in gold letters, though its most attractive feature is the central terrace facing the Eiffel Tower. Art that bows before Paris and with sapient modesty. The Tour Montparnasse and the Dôme des Invalides can be espied through the trees of its gardens, and some tower blocks in the 15th *arrondissement* are visible on the right. The Seine is very close by, but out of sight. The stage is thus held by the Eiffel Tower at the end of the symmetrical Champ-de-Mars, its thrust accentuated by the long, low silhouette of the Ecole Militaire that closes the picture.

◀ 0 | 90° | 180° | 270° | 315° ▶ 360°

36.

A. B.-V.

Die schönste Pariser Brücke, die Pont Alexandre III, erinnert mit ihrem Namen und ihrem Schmuck an die 1892 geschlossene Allianz zwischen Frankreich und Russland. Sie ist ein Emblem des Stahlzeitalters, ein barockes Revival, bedeckt mit Girlanden, Kandelabern, Meeresfiguren und Pflanzenmotiven. Der Zar selbst legte den Grundstein, eingeweiht wurde die Brücke jedoch 1900 von Nikolaus II., Sohn und Nachfolger Alexanders III. Geflügelte Pferde krönen die seitlichen Pylonen, passende Begleiter für einen weiteren Champion des neuen Eisenzeitalters, das sich von der Tyrannei der Formen befreit hat, vom Eiffelturm und dem Grand Palais mit seiner pagodenähnlichen Kuppel auf dem anderen Ufer – ein triumphierendes Relikt der Belle Époque. Der flach gespannte Bogen der Brücke scheint das Jahrhundert mit der fröhlichen Sorglosigkeit derer zu überziehen, die die Geschichte weniger fürchten als Zaren, Kaiserreiche und ihre Allianzen sowie die Epochen namens »Belles«.

From the Alexander III Bridge, the night steers the eye away from Les Invalides to explore other, more subtly conniving aerial paths of light the day denies. Emblem of the age of steel, this Baroque revival bedecked with garlands, candelabra, marine figures and plant motifs set out to celebrate the alliance formed by its namesake with France. It was he, indeed, who laid the first stone, whereas the bridge itself was inaugurated by his successor Nicholas II in 1900. Winged horses surmount the four-columned pedestals, fit companions for another champion of the new Iron Age with its release from the tyranny of forms, the Eiffel Tower, and the Grand Palais with its pointed, pagoda-like cupola on the other bank, a triumphant relic of the Belle Epoque. A bridge whose rugged arches span our century with the happy insouciance of one who fears history less than czars, empires and their alliances, and epochs yclept Beautiful.

◀ 0 | 90° | 180° | 270° | 315°

37.

E. F.

38.

A. B.-V.

Noch mehr steigende Pferde, der x-te Platz, der nach einem König benannt ist, in diesem Fall Ludwig XV. – die Place de la Concorde kann zumindest ein würdigeres Etikett verlangen. Der Platz

Yet more prancing horses, an umpteenth square named after a king, Louis XV this time round, the Place de la Concorde can at least claim that it deserves a more appropriate label. «Space» would

32.

A. B.-V.

Der Dôme des Invalides strahlt eine Autorität und einen Elan aus, der ihn zum Gegenstück des Schlosses von Versailles macht – die einzigartige Vermählung zwischen einem Stil, einer Epoche und einer Funktion. Die Kapelle mit ihrer Kuppel (110 m) wurde für Ludwig XIV. von dem jungen Hardouin-Mansart erbaut, der zweifellos wünschte, seinem Herrn ein Mausoleum zu schaffen, das mit seinen Ambitionen in Einklang stand. Dennoch ist es Napoleon, der die Massen in die Kapelle eines der wenigen Monumente zieht, denen das Grand Siècle seinen Namen verdankt.

Les Invalides draws in every line of horizontal force to rise yet higher in the sky with an authority and an elan that make it the counterpart of the castle of Versailles in a unique marriage between a style, an epoch and a function. The chapel with its dome (110 metres) was erected for Louis XIV by the young Jules Hardouin-Mansart, who no doubt thought to provide his master with a mausoleum commensurate with his ambitions, whereas it is Napoléon who draws the crowds in the chapel of one of the few monuments without which Le Grand Siècle would not have fully earned its name.

33.

A. B.-V.

Der Turm vibriert noch unter tausenden von Füßen und den Aufzügen, die im Licht des Vollmonds den Eiffelturm hinuntergehen beziehungsweise fahren. Was sehen die Besucher, die im Restaurant im zweiten Stock scherzen, oder jene, die mit dem Bus oder der Fähre in ihr Hotel zurückgebracht werden? Die Nacht erlöst das Symbol von Paris von seiner Pflicht als vertikale Promenade. Es entwickelt ein Eigenleben, behauptet seine Arroganz. Nur eine Nacht in dem kleinen Appartement, das Gustave Eiffel für sich im dritten Stock reserviert hatte, bietet die Möglichkeit, alles auszukosten, was der Turm nach Sonnenuntergang zu bieten hat.

A lighted tower for a Ville-lumière. A thousand feet and a dangle of lifts work their way up and down the Eiffel Tower in the moonlight. What do they see, those who dally in the second-floor restaurant, or those borne back to their hotels by bus or ferry? Night relieves this symbol of Paris of its duty to act as a vertical promenade. It acquires a life of its own, asserts its hauteur, its beckoning, yet distant finger. One night alone spent in the little apartment Gustave Eiffel set aside for himself on the third storey would be the only way to savour all that his tower experiences after the sun goes down.

34.

A. B.-V.

Alles Gold einer Pariser Nacht glitzert an den Statuen des Palais de Chaillot, das seinen Namen seit 1937 trägt, als es das ehemalige Palais du Trocadéro (1878) ersetzte. Welchen nächtlichen Kult erwarten die Vestalinen und Epheben? Die einzige bekleidete Statue blickt auf die Maske, die sie in Händen hält, und ein junger, lebendiger Gärtner trägt eine Gießkanne. Zwischen diesen beiden Figuren der Nacht, der lieblichen Flora gegenüber und den Gruppen »Joie de Vivre« und »Jeunesse« in den Gärten ragt der Eiffelturm majestätisch in den Himmel.

All the gold of a Parisian night glitters on the statues of the Palais de Chaillot, the name borne since 1937 by the building erected on the site of the former Palais du Trocadéro (1878). What nocturnal cult is awaited by these vestals and epheboi? The only draped figure lowers its eyes on the mask it holds. A young, lively gardener carries a heavy watering-can. Between these two *figurants*, the lovely Flora opposite, the Joie de Vivre and Youth groups in the gardens, and the sturdy, solid forms of those days offset the starkly soaring Eiffel Tower.

30.

E.F.

Meisterhaft oder pompös, ein Medley aller europäischen Stile, Vorläufer eines wahren Empirestils – die Pariser Oper wurde in jeder Hinsicht kritisch beurteilt. Als *Opus majus* des Zweiten Kaiserreichs, das unterging, bevor das Werk vollendet war, und als Meisterstück des jungen Architekten Charles Garnier ist die Oper mehr als nur eine Bühne. Sie ist selbst ein Spektakel, eine Melange aus Musik, Malerei und Rhetorik. Musen und Genies greifen in die Saiten der Lyren und künden bis unter den Giebel von der Grandeur lyrischer Kunst. Die Zeit ließ die Farben verblassen, die Garniers Palette entsprungen sind, als er seine farbigen Steine und Marmore, seine vergoldeten Statuen und seine Ornamente aus Bronze und Kupfer großzügig über das Gebäude verteilte. Das Treppenhaus, das Foyer de la Danse und die Prunkzimmer sind jedoch gut erhalten. Der Balettfreund tut gut daran, sich dem Luxus dieses Vergnügens hinzugeben und zu vergessen, dass die Oper einen Platz beherrscht, der zwar als seine Dienerin geschaffen wurde, gleichzeitig jedoch Ort des Bigbusiness, des Handels und der Banken ist, jener anderen Welt, für die Haussmann die Grands Boulevards und die Avenue de l'Opéra zerstörte, damit Arbeit und Vergnügen sich wie lustige Kumpanen auf der imperialen Bühne fühlen konnten.

Masterly or pompous, a medley of every European style, progenitor of a genuine Empire style, the Paris Opéra has received the full gamut of critical assessment. *Opus major* of a Second Empire that did not last long enough to see it completed, masterpiece of a young graduate in architecture, Charles Garnier (1825-98), the Opéra is something more than a place for shows. It is itself a spectacle, a mélange of music, painting and oratory. Muses and winged genii brandishing lyres proclaim the grandeur of lyric art right up to the gable. Time has sternly washed out some of the hues that sprang from Garnier's rainbow palette as he sprinkled his coloured stones and marbles, gilded statues and ornaments in bronze and copper over the building with a lavish hand. The great stairway, the Foyer de la Danse and the state apartments, however, have conserved their fires. The balletomane will do well to let himself sink into the pleasure of luxury trumpeted abroad as in a manifesto, and forget that the Opéra reigns over a square that was indeed designed as its handmaid, but is also the haunt of big business, trade, banks, that other world for which Haussmann hacked out the Grands Boulevards and the Avenue de l'Opéra so that work and pleasure could feel boon companions on the festive imperial stage.

◀ 0 | 90° | 180°

31.

A. B.-V.

La Madeleine, die Kirche im Stil eines griechischen Tempels, erhebt sich am Zusammenfluss der Grands Boulevards, dem Viertel des Showbusiness, mit der geschäftigen Rue Royal als Pendant zum Palais-Bourbon unweit der Place de la Concorde auf der anderen Seite der Seine. Das Gotteshaus ist der heiligen Maria Magdalena geweiht. Der feierlich klassische Mantel, der den Namen dieser reuigen Sünderin umhüllt, dient vielleicht dazu, das Bühnen- und Nachtvolk zu verführen, für das feierlicher Ernst eine notwendige Zierde ist, um erfolgreich zu sein. La Madeleine hat viele Begräbniszeremonien erlebt, von der Bestattung des korsischen Königs Carbone bis zu jener von Thierry Le Luron. Ganz Paris hat sich im Halbdunkel in ihre Bänke gequetscht, denn ihr Baumeister Vignon hielt am griechischen Modell fest, das keine Seitenbeleuchtung erlaubt; und das Licht von Paris entspricht bei weitem nicht jenem der Akropolis. Napoleon widmete diesen Tempel seiner Grande Armée und die Mysterien von Paris haben die Kirche zum irreligiösesten Gotteshaus gemacht, dessen Fassade noch nie ein Kreuz geziert hat, aber auch zum parisischsten.

The Greek temple church erected at the confluence of Les Grands Boulevards, the showbiz district, with the business-clad Rue Royale as a pendant to the Palais-Bourbon some way off beyond the Place de la Concorde on the other side of the Seine is known as La Madeleine, since it is dedicated to Mary Magdalene. The somewhat severe classical cloak wrapped around the name of this repentant sinner serves, perhaps, to seduce the stage and nocturnal folk, for whom solemnity is a necessary adornment to flourish in the face of life and death. A string of funerals from that of Carbone, a Corsican known as the king of the Pigalle, to that of a mimic, Thierry Le Luron, have huddled all Paris, and Paris as a whole, along its pews in semi-darkness, since the stern respect for Athens displayed by its architects forbade illumination from the side, and it need hardly be said that the light of Paris cannot hold a candle to that of the Acropolis. Napoleon associated La Madeleine with his Grande Armée, and the mysteries of Paris have conspired to make it both the least religious of all no cross has ever graced its façade – and one of the most Parisian of all – the city's churches.

◀ 0 | 90° | 180° | 270° | 315°

28.

A. B.-V.

Mit Betonung glasgefasster Arkaden, aber auch mit einem Gespür für den Dekor sind das Petit Palais und das Grand Palais seit beinahe einhundert Jahren unter dem arroganten Blick des Dôme des Invalides in einen wortlosen Dialog verstrickt. Ein stiller Dialog, erfüllt von Nostalgie und dem Verlangen nach einem neuen Jahrhundert, die Belle Époque, als Paris zum letzten Mal von sich selbst als Zentrum Europas träumen konnte, als Hauptstadt der Welt. Der Pomp und der Lebensstil, die Festivals, die Torheiten dieser Jahre reflektiert die Architektur der beiden Palais, die sich einreihen in die weltlichen Kathedralen des Industriezeitalters, des Zeitalters von Eisen und Stahl, berühmt durch Orsay und Saint-Lazare, die Bahnhöfe im Osten und Norden, und andere Zeugen entlang der Rue Réaumur. 1900, zur Zeit der Weltausstellung in Paris, forderte der Triumph der Industrie die Vermählung von Eisen und Glas mit Stein. Das Augenmerk richtete sich auf Strukturen, Treppen und Glasverkleidungen. Das monumentale Portal des Petit Palais, die riesige 43 m hohe Glasgallerie und das herrliche Treppenhaus des Grand Palais sind überschwängliche Meisterwerke, die ein Eigenleben führen. Die beiden Paläste, die so anders sind als die anderen, strahlen ein Gefühl der Lebensfreude und des Glücks aus.

With emphasis, yet with a clear sense of decoration, of glass-enclosed arcades, the Petit Palais and the Grand Palais have for nigh on a hundred years been engaged in a wordless dialogue under the haughty gaze of Les Invalides. A silent dialogue imbued with nostalgia, a yearning for the turn of the century, La Belle Époque, when for the last time Paris could dream of itself as the centre of Europe, the capital of the world. The pomp and circumstance, the festivals, the follies of these years are reflected in the architecture of these two Palais, which must be ranked with those lay cathedrals of the industrial age, the age of iron and steel, known as the Orsay, Saint-Lazare, East and North railway stations, the covered markets and other demonstration edifices along Rue Réaumur, especially their splendour. On the occasion of the 1900 Universal Exposition, the triumph of industry demanded the marriage of iron and glass with stone, hence the importance accorded to structure, stairways, glass panellings. The monumental porch of the Petit Palais, the immense glass gallery 43 metres high, and the fine staircase of the Grand Palais are exuberant masterpieces in their own right. A feeling of joie de vivre, of happiness, almost, yet a happiness that does not shrink before facile effects, emanates from these palaces so different from the rest.

29.

E. F.

Vor welchem Anblick bäumt sich das Pferd auf, das Ludwig XIV. mit einer Hand bändigt? Vielleicht versucht es dem erniedrigenden Schicksal seines Vorgängers zu entkommen, dessen Bronze 1792 eingeschmolzen wurde, um daraus das heutige Werk zu formen. Die Place des Victoires, der Platz, den einst der Duke de la Feuillade seinem Souverän darbot – wobei er sich selbst ruinierte –, hat viele Gründe, sich über städtische Revolutionen zu beklagen. Jene, die auf Haussmann folgten, rissen die herrlichen Villen nieder, die 1883 verhinderten, dass man in die Rue Etienne-Marcel gelangte. Damit war der Platz seiner Harmonie beraubt, die er der Hand Hardouin-Mansarts verdankte, der die Villen um die Statue in einheitlichem Stil kreiert hatte. Nahe dem Palais Royal, der Galerie Colbert, dem Zentrum der Fertigkleidungsbranche, in dem die neuen Häuser errichtet wurden, bleibt die Place des Victoires ein schönes Beispiel für die städtische Ordnung, die die königlichen Plätze dem Paris des 17. und 18. Jahrhunderts aufdrängten.

At the centre of the circle of elegant women, of mannequins and their favourite creators, towards which flashing view is this horse rearing, held in check by Louis XIV with one hand? Perhaps it is seeking to flee the degrading destiny of its predecessor, whose bronze was melted down in 1792 to be replaced by the present work. The Place des Victoires, the square offered to his sovereign by the original Duke de la Feuillade, who ruined himself in the process, had much to reason to complain about urban revolutions. Those who came after Haussmann demolished those of the fine mansions that prevented the opening the Rue Etienne-Marcel in 1883. The square was thus shorn of the harmony it had received at the hands of Hardouin-Mansart (1646-1708), who designed its strictly similar mansions all around the central statue. Close to the Palais-Royal, the Galerie Colbert, centre of the designer styled ready-to-wear trade, where the new fashion houses have taken up residence, the Place des Victoires remains a fine example of the «new urban» order the royal squares imposed on 17th and 18th-century Paris.

53.

A. B.-V.

Was wäre Montmartre ohne seine Maler? In der ersten Dekade dieses Jahrhunderts kamen Dutzende hierher auf der Suche nach Aufträgen, auf der Suche nach etwas Genialem. Utrillos Selle hat nie etwas anderes gekannt als diese Szenen. Eines Tages, als eine Inspiration den Hunger begleitete, gebar Picasso am Bâteau-Lavoir nicht nur »Des Demoiselles d'Avignon«, sondern auch den Kubismus. Van Dongen zog aus, um sein Glück zu suchen, Juan Gris stand an der Schwelle zum Tod. Als der Hügel zum In-Platz wurde, flüchteten die meisten Künstler ans andere Ufer der Seine. Dennoch ist etwas von jenen geblieben, die hier lebten, liebten und arbeiteten, die ihr Genie und ihre Jugend erschöpften. Was macht es schon, wenn der Großteil der Gemälde, die zum Kauf angeboten werden, von südostasiatischen Akkordarbeitern produziert wird, die Montmartre noch nicht einmal von einer Postkarte kennen? Montmartre ist aus den Flügeln der Kunst und der Malerei geboren: Vom »Lapin Agile« bis zum »Bal du Moulin de la Galette«, von der Rue Ravignan bis zum Bâteau-Lavoir trifft man überall am Hügel auf die doppelte Maske aus Realität und Bühnenbild. Vielleicht ist Montmartre selbst nur Schein ...

What would Montmartre be without its painters? In the first decade of this century, there were dozens stumping the streets in search of a commission, in search of the touch of genius, whether in their studios or in their cups, whose palette can always be relied upon to give life a rosy glow. Utrillo's soul never saw other scenes than these. At the Bateau-Lavoir, one day when hunger consorted with inspiration, Picas so gave birth to both «Les Demoiselles d'Avignon», and cubism. Van Dongen departed to find fame and fortune, Juan Gris came close to death's door. When the Butte became the in place, most of these artists hightailed it to the other side of the Seine. Yet something has survived of those who lived, loved and toiled here, who wore out their genius and the proud vanguard of their youth. What matter if the bulk of the canvases offered to the blind eagerness of the gullible are churned out by an assembly line of Southeast Asian pieceworkers who have never even seen Montmartre on a picture postcard? Montmartre was born and got off the ground on the wings of art and painting: from the Lapin Agile to the Bal du Moulin de la Galette, from Rue Ravignan to the Bateau-Lavoir, the whole of the Butte is affected by this double guise imposed by reality and a stage setting. Perhaps the place itself is a *trompe-l'œil.*

54.

A. B.-V.

Über den Bäumen, über den dicht gedrängten Dächern am Butte Montmartre, über den Glasmauern und Ateliers thront die Sacré-Cœur, die Paris eine exotische Mischung aus Moschee und byzantinischer Kultur schenkt. Ihr Scheitel befindet sich auf gleicher Höhe wie der Butte Chaumont. Per Dekret einer Nationalversammlung, die überwiegend aus Provinzlern bestand, wurde die Kirche ab 1876 als Sühne für den Sittenverfall errichtet, der 1870 zur Niederlage Frankreichs geführt hatte. Man stülpte den destruktiven sozialen und ökonomischen Leidenschaften, die in der Brust des Paris des ausgehenden Jahrhunderts schlugen und noch einmal die französische Gesellschaft zu Fall bringen konnten, hoffnungsvoll einen Deckel über. Er hielt jedoch der Revolution des Kubismus und den gewaltigen Protesten des Fauvismus nicht stand, die zu jener Explosion führten, die Europa 1914 erschütterte. Ihre Schöpfer arbeiteten besser, als sie ahnten, und heute gehört die Sacré-Cœur zu den bekanntesten Bildern von Paris.

Above the trees, above the crowded roofs that climb the Butte Montmartre, above the walls of glass and the ateliers, the Sacré-Cœur has grafted an exotic blend of mosques and Byzantium from the Middle East onto Paris. Its summit is flush with the Butte Chaumont, but is essentially a summit of the imaginary. Decreed in 1873 by a National Assembly very largely composed of provincials, the basilica was erected in expiation of the slump in morals that had led to France's defeat in 1870. The lid thus hopefully placed on the destructive social and economic passions that lurked in the breast of *fin-de-siècle* Paris and might once again have brought French society to the ground, was no match for the revolution of cubism and the violent hues of fauvism, let alone the explosion that rocked Europe in 1914. Its creators, however, built better than they knew, and the Sacré-Cœur has become one of the best known images of Paris.

55.

A. B.-V.

Das Restaurant ist italienisch, die umliegenden Häuser sind nagelneu und gehören zur Luxusklasse. Hier fand der berühmteste Ball des Montmartre statt, der jeden Sonntag Fabrikarbeiterinnen, Näherinnen und Büglerinnen anzog. Ihr Lachen und ihr Geschnatter unter den Bäumen berührte die Herzen der jungen Herren am Butte. Renoir machte den Ball im »Moulin de la Gallette« unsterblich, ein Fest, das Symbol für Lebensfreude war, für das lebendige, ausgelassene Paris, das die Pinsel der Impressionisten entflammte. Keines der rauen Merkmale des »Moulin Rouge«, wie es Toulouse-Lautrec sah. Drama stand nicht auf der Karte, sondern das frische, reine Vergnügen einer populären Fete. Das Symbol ist geblieben, ebenso wie die für Montmartre typische Galanterie.

The restaurant is Italian, the houses around are brand new and of the luxury class. This was the most renowned of the Bals de Montmartre that summoned factory girls, sempstresses and ironing women every Sunday. Beneath the trees, their giggling and twitterings stirred the manly hearts of the young dwellers on the Butte. The dancing place of the Moulin de la Gallette immortalised by Renoir was the symbol of the *joie de vivre*, the lively, gay Paris that enflamed the brushes of the Impressionists. None of the harsh traits of the Moulin-Rouge as seen by Toulouse-Lautrec. Drama was not on the menu. The fresh, sincere joy of a popular fete. The symbol has remained, along with a tradition of gallantry that has stuck with Montmartre.

56.

A. B.-V.

Die Haltestation Abbesses der Métro scheint der einzige erhaltene »Kristallpalast« von Paris zu sein. Hector Guimard führte einen Stil ein, der Metall an der Wende des Stahlzeitalters in den Vordergrund rückte. Die Äbtissinnen von Montmartre spielten in der lokalen Geschichte eine bedeutende Rolle. Eine erwarb sogar die Gunst Heinrichs IV. Der letzte seiner Linie, blind und taub, wurde guillotiniert. Man hatte ihn des schweren Verbrechens beschuldigt, »taub und blind« gegen die Republik komplottiert zu haben. Die Eminenzen in ihren handgesponnenen Roben sind heute vergessen, der Jugendstil ist noch immer lebendig. Er gibt der Station Atmosphäre. Lianen, Stämme, ineinander verwobenen Zweige und skizzierte Blumen verleihen jedem Mobiliar einen mysteriösen, femininen Charme, eine verwirrende Anmut. Über welchen verschütteten Wäldern, über welchen verbotenen Gärten öffnet sich dieses ratternde Maul? Tief in seinem Innern verbirgt Paris einen vegetabilischen Traum. Durch Guimards Magie hat der Traum Gestalt angenommen, modern und so vergnüglich wie immer.

The Metro's Abbesses station (once should say that of the Metropolitan railway) seems to be the only one of Paris's «crystal palaces» left. It was Hector Guimard who invented a style that led metal to the top at the turn of our century of steel. The abbesses of Montmartre were of great importance in its local history. One won the favour of the ebullient Henry IV. The last of the line, blind and deaf, was guillotined during the Terror on the weighty charge of having «deafly and blindly» plotted against the Republic. These eminences in their homespun robes are now forgotten, whereas art nouveau is still alive. It gave the station its air, a genre whose decorative vitality was the stuff of dreams. Lianas, trunks, softly interwoven branches, sketched flowers, a supple plant elan conferred on furniture of every kind a mysterious, feminine charm, a disturbing grace. On what buried forests, on what secret gardens does this rumbling maw open? Deep down in its innards, Paris hides a vegetal dream. Guimard's magic has made that dream take form, modern and as pleasurable as ever.